LAST WORDS SERIES

Life, Death & Last Words of The Musical Genius

FRANZ PETER SCHUBERT

DR. ANUP KUMAR CHANDA

BLUEROSE PUBLISHERS
U.K.

Copyright © Anup Kumar Chanda 2025

All rights reserved by author. No part of this publication may be reproduced, stored in a retrieval system or transmitted in any form or by any means, electronic, mechanical, photocopying, recording or otherwise, without the prior permission of the author. Although every precaution has been taken to verify the accuracy of the information contained herein, the publisher assumes no responsibility for any errors or omissions. No liability is assumed for damages that may result from the use of information contained within.

BlueRose Publishers takes no responsibility for any damages, losses, or liabilities that may arise from the use or misuse of the information, products, or services provided in this publication.

For permissions requests or inquiries regarding this publication, please contact:

BLUEROSE PUBLISHERS
www.BlueRoseONE.com
info@bluerosepublishers.com
+4407342408967

ISBN: 978-93-7018-825-9

Cover design: Daksh
Typesetting: Tanya Raj Upadhyay

First Edition: February 2025

To

My loving wife

Dhriti

whose constant inspiration made it possible

for me to write this book

"Mozart and Beethoven are geniuses, but Schubert is a miracle."

-- Brian Newbould

About the author

An alumnus of the Indian Statistical Institute, Kolkata, Dr. Anup Kumar Chanda joined the Indian Administrative Service in 1976 and was allotted to West Bengal Cadre.

A winner of Rafael Lusky Prize in Economics, Dr. Chanda was declared the most outstanding graduate student by the Department of Economics, University of Florida, Gainesville, USA and was invited to become a member of the prestigious Phi Kappa Phi Honor Society, USA in 1984 based on his scholastic achievement.

After working with both the Central and the State Governments in various capacities, Dr. Chanda joined as Chairman, Kolkata Port Trust in 2002 and worked as such till 2009, and also as Chairman of the Indian Ports Association from 2007 to 2009. He also worked as Additional Chief Secretary, Government of West Bengal and thereafter as Member of the West Bengal Administrative Tribunal till 2018.

Preface

In the grand tapestry of musical history, certain names shine with a brilliance that transcends the passage of time. Among these luminaries, Franz Peter Schubert occupies a hallowed place as a true poet of melody. Born into a world of cultural change and artistic revolution, Schubert's short life was a testament to the power of music to capture the essence of human emotion and to transcend the limitations of earthly existence.

Schubert was an Austrian composer born in 1797 and considered one of the greatest composers of the early Romantic era. He composed over 600 vocal works, seven complete symphonies, sacred music, operas, incidental music, and a large body of chamber and piano music. Some of his most famous works include the "*Unfinished Symphony*," the "*Trout Quintet*," the song cycle "*Winterreise*," and hundreds of Lieder (German art songs).

Despite his short life (he died at 31), Schubert's compositions are celebrated for their lyrical melodies, harmonic innovation, and emotional depth. His influence on subsequent composers, particularly in the development of the German Lied, is profound.

Schubert's life was marked by several interesting events and facets:

Early Musical Talent: Schubert showed remarkable musical talent from a young age. He began learning the violin and piano as a child, and his early compositions, even as a teenager, demonstrated his gift for melody and harmony.

Friendship with Beethoven: Schubert idolized Beethoven and was fortunate to meet him in Vienna. Beethoven recognized Schubert's talent and even received some of his compositions. There's a famous anecdote that Beethoven listened to one of Schubert's songs and exclaimed, ""*Truly, the spark of divine genius resides in this Schuber*t!"

Prolific Composer: Despite dying young at the age of 31, Schubert composed a vast amount of music. He left behind over 600 secular vocal works (including more than 600 Lieder), seven complete symphonies, sacred music, operas, incidental music, and a large body of chamber and piano music. His productivity was extraordinary, with many of his compositions written in a short span of time.

The Unfinished Symphony: One of Schubert's most famous works is his Symphony No. 8 in B minor, commonly known as the "*Unfinished Symphony*." Schubert began composing it in 1822 but only completed two movements. The reason for its unfinished state remains a mystery, but these two movements are considered some of his finest orchestral writing.

Lieder and Song Cycles: Schubert revolutionized the Lied (German art song), elevating it to a form of high art. He composed numerous Lieder, setting poetry to music with exceptional sensitivity to the text. His song cycles, such as "*Die schöne Müllerin*" and "*Winterreise*," are masterpieces that explore themes of love, nature, and existential despair.

Schubert's health was fragile throughout his life. He suffered (most probably) from syphilis, which likely contributed to his early death. Despite his health struggles, Schubert maintained a wide circle of friends in Vienna's artistic and intellectual circles and was known for his sociable nature and love of gathering with friends for music-making sessions (*Schubertiads*).

Posthumous Recognition: Schubert's music gained broader recognition after his death. His brother, Ferdinand, and friends worked diligently to publish and promote his works posthumously. His compositions had a significant influence on later Romantic composers such as Mendelssohn, Schumann, Brahms, and Liszt.

Schubert's life highlights not only his musical genius but also the challenges and personal experiences that shaped his compositions and legacy.

****

Franz Schubert, though often overshadowed by contemporaries like Mozart and Beethoven and later composers like Brahms and Wagner, occupies a unique place in the history of music. Here's a comparison of Schubert with some of these composers:

Mozart

Mozart's style is characterized by elegance, clarity, and a sense of balance. His melodies are graceful and refined, blending classical forms with a playful and charming quality. Mozart's music tends to exhibit a sense of perfection in its structure and harmonic language, showcasing his technical mastery and creativity. Schubert, on his part, is known for his lyrical and expressive melodies, and excelled in creating poignant and emotionally rich music. His gift for melody, particularly in his Lieder and song cycles, is unparalleled. Schubert's music often evokes a sense of intimacy and introspection, exploring themes of love, nature, and human existence with a deep emotional resonance.

Schubert, on his part, was adept at classical forms such as sonata form and symphony; his approach was more fluid and less rigid compared to Mozart. Schubert's compositions often feature unexpected harmonic shifts, expressive modulations, and a willingness to explore new harmonic territories, particularly in his later works.

Mozart enjoyed widespread acclaim and recognition during his lifetime as a child prodigy and later as a mature composer. His operas, symphonies, chamber music, and piano works were celebrated across Europe, and he was highly esteemed by both audiences and fellow musicians. In contrast, Schubert's recognition was more limited during his lifetime. He was known primarily within Vienna's artistic circles and among his close friends, although he did achieve some success with his Lieder. His reputation as a composer grew significantly after his death, thanks to the efforts of his friends and supporters, and his compositions and music have a lasting influence on subsequent generations of composers in their works.

In fine, while both Mozart and Schubert were masters of melody and composition, their styles and impacts differed in terms of their approach to form, their reception during their lifetimes, and their lasting influence on subsequent generations of composers.

Beethoven:

Beethoven's music is known for its heroic and dramatic qualities, pushing the boundaries of form and expression. His symphonies, sonatas, and concertos are monumental and revolutionary.

Beethoven's influence on Schubert was profound, with Schubert idolizing him and attempting to follow in his footsteps. However, Schubert's style is generally more lyrical and intimate compared to Beethoven's grandeur.

Mendelssohn:

Mendelssohn's music often combines Classical structure with Romantic lyricism. He was known for his clear forms, elegant melodies, and a sense of balance between intellect and emotion.

Mendelssohn admired Schubert's works and helped to revive interest in them after Schubert's death. However, compared to Schubert, Mendelssohn's compositions are typically more polished and cosmopolitan, reflecting his upbringing and education.

Schumann:

Schumann's music is characterized by its introspective nature, imaginative use of harmony, and a strong sense of literary and emotional expression. His piano works and songs are particularly esteemed.

Schumann was deeply influenced by Schubert's Lieder and song cycles. Both composers shared a similar lyrical and introspective approach to music, though Schumann's compositions often exhibit a more intricate and complex texture.

Brahms:

Brahms' music is known for its structural integrity, rich harmonies, and mastery of counterpoint. He often embraced Classical forms while incorporating Romantic expressiveness.

Brahms respected Schubert's achievements but his own compositions had a more rigorous and formal approach. While Schubert's works are more spontaneous and lyrical, Brahms' compositions often exhibit a more deliberate and intellectual approach.

Wagner:

Wagner's music is revolutionary in its use of leitmotifs, chromaticism, and the concept of the '*Gesamtkunstwerk*' (total work of art). His operas are monumental and deeply influenced by Romantic philosophy.

Wagner's impact on music and opera was immense, contrasting with Schubert's more modest scale and focus on Lieder, chamber music, and symphonies. Wagner's operatic innovations marked a departure from the traditions Schubert worked within.

In summary, Schubert's music stands out for its lyricism, emotional depth, and mastery of the Lied. While he didn't push the frontiers of musical form and structure as boldly as some of his contemporaries and successors, his ability to express profound human emotions through melody and harmony ensures his enduring legacy in the Romantic era and beyond.

****

Born in Vienna in 1797, Schubert's prodigious talent was evident from an early age. His music, infused with lyrical beauty and emotional depth, became an emblem of the early Romantic era, where artistic expression embraced the individual spirit. His gift for melody was unparalleled, allowing him to capture the most profound human sentiments within the confines of notes and chords. Through intimate Lieder and grand symphonic works, Schubert transported listeners to worlds of tender love, existential contemplation, and unbridled joy.

This book seeks to highlight the life, music, and spirit of this extraordinary composer who, despite a premature death at the tender age of 31, bequeathed a legacy that reverberates through the corridors of musical history. In the pages that follow, we embark on a journey that explore the rich tapestry of Schubert's life, uncover the events that shaped his art, delve into the beauty of his compositions, and also capture his tragic death along with his last words.

■■■

This book is dedicated to my loving wife Dhriti whose constant inspiration and encouragement made it possible for me to undertake this venture.

Let me also acknowledge my debt to my parents, Late Bibhuti Bhusan Chanda and Late Binapani Chanda for their constant love, affection and support in my life that made me what I'm today, and gave me the courage to undertake new ventures in life. I am also grateful to our son-in-law Sourabh, daughter Sagnika and our granddaughter Pakhi (Jonaki) for their love and affection that gave me the strength to go forward with the present venture. I also gratefully acknowledge the constant encouragement I received from my elder brother Shri Pradip Kumar Chanda, without which this book would not have been possible.

With this, let me welcome the readers, one and all, to the world of Franz Peter Schubert, the musical genius, who, though overshadowed in fame during his own time, emerged as a towering figure in the annals of musical history. He was, as rightly said by the celebrated English composer, conductor and author Brian Newbould, indeed a *'miracle'* whose music, with its poignancy and profound emotional resonance, continues to inspire and stir the hearts of generations to come.[1]

24 January 2025 (Dr. Anup Kumar Chanda)

---

[1] "*Mozart and Beethoven are geniuses, but Schubert is a miracle.*" -- Brian Newbould

Prologue

His Last words

Franz Peter Schubert (31 January 1797 -- 19 November 1828)

"No, no. It is not true. This is not Beethoven lying here!"

Franz Peter Schubert

He had just returned from Styria – the beautiful mountainous, forested state in southern Austria, known for its wine, spas and castles – and was planning to go for another trip in the autumn of 1828, to restore his health weakened by constant headache, indisposition; but still there was no sign of the imminent catastrophe.

On 1 September he moved from his friend Schober's place into an apartment rented by his brother Ferdinand in a new building in Neu-Wieden, a new suburb to the south-west of Vienna. The move was advised by his doctor; but the humidity of the new building and the insanitary conditions in the new suburb were anything but healthy.

It was in September 1828 he began to feel the approach of illness. He was becoming increasingly weak and giddy; the doctors advised him moderation and exercise in the open air. He followed their advice; and it certainly raised his spirits.

About 5 October he took a three-day walking tour with Ferdinand and two other friends to visit Unterwaltersdorf, a village in the city of Ebreichsdortf in Lower Austria, and Haydn's grave in Eisenstadt, a small Austrian city in Burgenland, on the plain leading down to the river Wulka, at the south foot of the Leitha Mountains, close to the Hungarian border.– a round trip of over 100 km.

But, on his return to Vienna, he became ill once again. While dining at a tavern on the last day of October, he suddenly threw his knife and fork down onto the plate, and said the fish he had just begun eating filled him with a sensation of disgust and horror, as though he had taken poison. From this time forward, he scarcely ate and drank anything and took only medicines.

On 3 November he set off early in the morning and walked from Neu-Wieden to the Parish Church in Hernals, the picturesque town bordering the Vienna Woods, a three-hour walk, to listen to a performance of a Latin requiem, composed by his brother Ferdinand, the last music that he ever heard.

Returning home, he complained of weariness. A few days later, weakness confined him to bed; and with each passing day, his condition worsened. The syphilitic infection which he had contracted about five years earlier was apparently taking its toll and was now in its final phase.

The musical genius Schubert, the "King of lied", was dying.[2]

By 11 November he became seriously ill, and gave up the struggle to walk his way through the illness.

---

[2] 'lied' is a type of German song, especially of the romantic period, typically for solo voice with piano accompaniment

He was lovingly and carefully nursed by his family, particularly by his sister, Maria. His close friend, Josef von Spaun wrote:

> *"I found him ill in bed although his condition did not seem to me at all serious. He corrected my copy in bed and was glad to see me and said, 'there is really nothing the matter with me, I'm so exhausted I feel as if I were going to fall through the bed'. He was cared for most affectionately by a charming thirteen-year old sister whom he praised very highly to me. I left him without any anxiety at all and it came as a thunderbolt when, a few days later, I heard of his death."*

On 12 November Schubert wrote his last letter --- to his friend Schober:

> *"I am ill. I have eaten nothing for eleven days and drunk nothing, and I totter feebly and shakily from my chair to bed and back again. Rinna is treating me. If ever I take anything, I bring it up at once.*
>
> *Be so kind, then, as to assist me in this desperate situation by means of literature. Of Cooper's I have read The Last of the Mohicans, The Spy, The Pilot and The Pioneers. If by any chance you have anything else of his, I implore you to deposit it with Frau von Bogner at the coffee-house for me. My brother, who is conscientiousness itself, will most faithfully pass it on to me. Or anything else."*

Till 12 November Schubert kept working; he was composing an opera and correcting the proofs of his song cycle "*Die Winterreise*" – but thereafter he could do no more. When friends visited to keep him company, he spoke about his next opera, and mentioned that he would like to listen to Beethoven's last quartet.

Two days later, Schubert, now bedridden, was deeply moved when the *Schuppanzigh* Quartet, of the noted violinist Ignaz Schuppanzigh, played for him Beethoven's C sharp minor String Quartet, Op 131. *"The King of Harmony has sent the King of Song a friendly bidding to the crossing*", said Karl Holz, one of the violinists who played it for him.

That day the doctor diagnosed '*advanced disintegration of the blood corpuscles*'.

On 17 November his friends, Bauernfeld and Lachner, visited him and found him alert; but that evening a delirium set in.

On 18 November he became increasingly delirious; he was raving violently. It was difficult to restrain him on the bed.[3]

Ferdinand described Schubert's last hours in a letter to his father, written two days after his death:

> *"On the evening before his death, though only half-conscious, he still said to me, 'I implore you to transfer me to my room, not to leave me here in this corner under the earth. Do I, then, deserve no place above the earth?' I answered him, dear Franz, rest assured, believe me, believe your brother Ferdinand, whom you have always trusted and who loves you so much, you are in the room which you have always been in so far and lie in your bed!"*

Schubert wanted to go out; he seemed to be under the impression that he was in a strange room. He thought he was being buried alive and felt himself close to Beethoven's grave; Beethoven – whom he adored throughout his life.

The doctor came and tried to reassure him; said he would recover if he stayed quietly in bed. But delirious from the effect of the fever, Schubert cried out to the physician: "*Here, here is my end.*" Later, he asked to be placed in his own bed. When assured that he already was there, in his delirious state, he exclaimed:

> "*No, no. It is not true. This is not Beethoven lying here!*"

---

[3] Bogousslavsky, Julien, Hennerici, M. G., Baezner, H., Bassetti, C. (Ed.): "*Neurological Disorders in Famous Artists*", Part 3, Karger, 2010, p. 76-77.

These were his last words. [4]

The following day, 19 November, after more delirium, at three in the afternoon, he breathed his last.

Schubert came to this world on a short visit. He was only 31 when he died.

****

Robert Schumann, the famous German composer, was an ardent admirer of Schubert. He is said to have *"cried all night"* when, at the age of 18, he heard of Schubert's death. In a tribute to the great maestro who was no more, Schumann said:

> *"Schubert, whose name, I thought, should only be whispered at night to the trees and stars.... will always remain the favourite of youth...Time, though producing much that is beautiful, will not soon produce another Schubert".*

In the words of Schumann, *"Schubert's pencil was dipped in moonbeams and in the flame of the sun!"*

Liszt described him as *"...the most poetic musician who ever lived".*

---

[4] Lewis Jr., Joseph W.: *"Last and Near-Last Words of the Famous, Infamous and Those In-Between"*, published by Author House, 2016.

Table of Contents

Franz Peter Schubert – Life & Music

Chapter 1 Early Years 1

Chapter 2 At the Stadtkonvikt 6

Chapter 3 Schubert leaves Stadtkonvikt – joins his father's school as a teacher 12

Chapter 4 The Musical journey: Early years (1814-1819) 14

Chapter 5 Schubert's friends: Friends in need 24

Chapter 6 The Musical Journey: The Middle years (1820-1824) 35

Chapter 7 The Musical journey – Later years (1825-1827) 70

Chapter 8 Schubert's Last Year (1828) 95

Chapter 9 Schubert's Music: Recognition 106

Chapter 10 Schubert & Other Vintage Virtuosi 109

Chapter 11 Schubert: The man within 129

Chapter 12 Schubert: Love & Romance 134

Chapter 13 Sex life of Franz Schubert 139

Chapter 14 Schubert's faith 152

Chapter 15 Death of Franz Schubert 156

Chapter 16 The Mystery surrounding Schubert's death 158

Chapter 17 The Last wish of Franz Schubert 167

Chapter 18 Funeral 171

Chapter 19 Schubert's Epitaph 174

Chapter 20 Schubert: The 'Phoenix' that rose from the ashes 179

Chapter 21 "*Zentralfriedhof*" in Vienna: The final resting place of Franz Schubert 186

Chapter 22 The king is dead, long live the king! Schubert immortalized after death 189

Chapter 23 Schubert's Footprints: Now Museums/Memorials in Vienna 193

Chapter 24 Schubert - A century later 199

Chapter 25 Epilogue 202

References 204

Franz Peter Schubert:
Life and Music
Chapter 1
Early Years

Schubert: "The King of lied"

Many great authors and artists became famous only after their death. John Keats, Edgar Allan Poe, Henry David Thoreau, and the famous painter Vincent van Gogh – to name a few--- all had gone the way of all flesh before gaining serious recognition. The Austrian composer Franz Schubert is another such genius who was overlooked in life but whose stock has grown with time.

Heralded as the "King of lied", Austrian Composer Franz Peter Schubert is enshrined as a pillar of Romantic Western Classical Music, who follows after Beethoven. Noted for the melody and harmony in his songs (lieder), piano pieces and chamber music, his compositions are unique as they bridged the worlds of Classical and Romantic music

Franz Peter Schubert

Born in Vienna in the last years of the 18th century, Schubert came of age in a period of artistic revolution. It was a time when the Enlightenment had set Europe ablaze with revolution and war. The essence and spirit of the era also had its reflection in the works of the contemporary artists, poets, writers, and composers in their expression of emotion and beauty. It was in this backdrop the Romantic Movement dominated the 19th century and gave birth to many of the world's greatest works of art.

The rise of the Romantic school involves a greater freedom in form, a fuller play of poetry and imagination, a general artistic evolution and independence in comparison with the form signifying the Classical period. This came about through Beethoven's sonata and symphonies as against the more Classic forms of Haydn and Mozart. The first major departure from the Classic tradition was made by Schubert, whose influence has been permanent in the development of Romanticism.

The 'King' is born

The Schubert family came originally from the province of Zukmantel in Austrian Silesia. In the year 1784, Schubert's father, Franz Theodor Schubert, came to Vienna to study, and his brother Carl, at that time a school teacher in the Leopoldstadt suburb, admitted him as an assistant. Two years after, he became schoolteacher in a parish in Lichtental in the suburb of Vienna. His wife, Elisabeth Vietz, the daughter of a Silesian locksmith, was a cook. She bore him fourteen children of whom only five survived; and after her death, Franz Sr. married a second wife, Anna Klayenbok, who bore him five more.

Franz Theodor Schubert   Elisabeth Vietz

Born on 31 January 1797, Schubert was the youngest of the four sons by the first marriage. His elder brothers were Ignaz, Karl, and Ferdinand; and there was a younger sister, Maria Theresa. The family was musical and cultivated string quartet playing at home -- the boy Franz playing the viola.

The house in which Schubert was born bears the sign of the Red Crab and is known as the '*Red Crayfish*'. It is marked by a grey marble plaque, with the inscription "Franz Schubert's Geburtshaus" (birth house) -- with a lyre on the right, and a wreath of laurel with the date of his birth on the left. This memorial was put up by the Choral Union of Vienna and was inaugurated in 1858. Besides this, a street leading into the Nussdorfer Strasse is named after the composer.

When Schubert was born, Beethoven was 27 years old. Mozart had died about five years earlier.

When he was just seven, his vocal talent was recognized by the famous composer Antonio Salieri, a contemporary of Mozart, the Austrian imperial Kapellmeister (music director), who lauded the boy Franz as a musical genius.

Early lessons

At the age of five, Schubert began to receive regular instruction from his father who played cello. Being a musical prodigy, it was not long before Schubert exceeded him.

For development of his instrumental skills, his brother Ignaz – 14 years older than Franz– was roped in to give him piano lessons, presumably in the young Schubert's 'eighth year', when the child's hands were a bit bigger. But, after a few months Ignaz had to give up, hopelessly outclassed, for his little brother could work the rest out better on his own. As narrated by Ignaz:

Ignaz Schubert

> *"I was amazed when Franz told me, a few months after we began, that he had no need of any further instruction from me, and that for the future he would make his own way. And in truth his progress in a short period was so great that I was forced to acknowledge in him a master who was far beyond me, one whom I could never catch up."*

As Schubert grew up, he was sent for singing lessons to Michael Holzer, the choir-master at the neighbourhood church in Liechtental. Holzer had a close relationship with the Schubert family. He did everything required of him to prepare young Schubert for the great moment.

Looking back in 1829 after his son's death, Schubert's father, Franz Sr. remembered those times mournfully, but proudly:

> *"When he was eight, I gave him preliminary instruction on the violin, and let him practise till he could play easy duets pretty well. After that I sent him for singing lessons to Michael Holzer, Choirmaster in Liechtental. He told me on several occasions, with tears in his eyes, that he had never had such a pupil. 'Whenever I tried to tell him something new, he already knew it. In consequence, I never really gave him lessons, just spoke to him and silently marvelled at him."*

In spite of his generous admission of Schubert's genius, it is certain that Holzer did give him instruction in thorough bass in playing the pianoforte and the organ. On one occasion, when he had given his pupil a theme, he was quite in ecstasy at the way he worked it out, and exclaimed, "*The boy has harmony in his little finger!*"

Schubert was a prodigy comparable only to Mozart --- Mozart who wrote a concerto for the piano at the age of six and at the age of eight an orchestral symphony. But after Mozart, Schubert is unrivalled. [5][6]

---

[5] Kreissle von Hellborn, Heinrich: "*The Life of Franz Schubert, Vol. 1*", Translated by Coleridge, Arthur Duke, Cambridge University Printing House, Cambridge, UK, 2014.

[6] Baltzell, Winton James: "*A Complete History of Music for Schools, Clubs, and Private Readings*", published by the Library of Alexandria, August 28, 2017.

Chapter 2
At the Stadtkonvikt

Salieri teaches Schubert

In 1808, Schubert was awarded a scholarship to study at the '*Stadtkonvikt*' -- the Imperial Seminary -- which trained young vocalists to become singers at the chapel of the Imperial Court. There he received lessons from Wenzel Ruzicka, the imperial court organist, and later from the renowned composer Antonio Salieri, the Austrian imperial Kapellmeister (music director) and a contemporary of Mozart, then at the height of his fame.

Antonio Salieri

At Stadtkonvikt, Schubert became acquainted with the orchestral music of Haydn, Mozart and Beethoven. He sang in the choir, played violin in the orchestra and learned musical theory and composition from none other than Salieri himself.

'Stadtkonvikt –Vienna, where Schubert as a choir boy took lessons from Antonio Salieri.

Salieri was a brilliant teacher and, under his direction, the young Schubert composed his first string quartets, songs, and piano pieces. At the age of 11, Schubert participated as a singer in the court-chapel choir directed by Salieri. He played violin in the students' orchestra; before long he was promoted to leader, and conducted in Ruzicka's absence. He also attended choir practice and, with his fellow pupils, practiced chamber music and piano playing.

Schubert was deep in penury; and the finance available was inadequate for a comfortable living.

In his early youth, he wrote a heart-rending letter to his brother Ferdinand:

> *"You know by experience how sometimes one wants to eat a roll and a few apples and all the more when after a modest dinner one can only look forward to a wretched supper eight and a half hours later."*

In his letter, Schubert asks for "only a few kreuzers a month, quotes the Bible in support of charity and closes pleadingly".

At the Stadtkonvikt, Schubert developed close friendship with Josef von Spaun; and it lasted throughout his life. In those early days, the financially well-off Spaun helped him in all possible ways, particularly with much of the manuscript paper he needed. In1814, he introduced Schubert to the poet Johann Mayrhofer.

Josef von Spaun

Schubert was a prolific composer. *"I work every morning,"* he said, *"When I have finished one new piece, I begin another."* He composed almost as rapidly as a copyist could set down the notes on paper. He once wrote fifteen songs in two days. The lied *"Hark, Hark, the Lark!"* based on Shakespeare's 'Cymbeline' was literally written on the back of a bill of fare.

Legend has it on a Sunday, during the summer of 1826, Schubert with several friends was returning from Pötzleinsdorf to the Vienna, and on strolling along through Währing, he saw his friend Ludwig Titze sitting at a table in a local beer garden. Schubert and his friends halted there in their journey for a drink and chat. Titze had a book of Shakespeare lying open before him, and Schubert soon began to turn over the leaves, and after skimming through 'Cymbeline', he suddenly exclaimed: "*A lovely melody has come into my head—if only I had some music paper!*"; whereupon one of his friends Franz Doppler "*drew a few music lines on the back of a bill of fare, and in the midst of a genuine Sunday hubbub, with fiddlers, skittle players, and waiters running about in different directions with orders, Schubert wrote that lovely song*".

The same day based on a text drawn from the Shakespeare comedy "*Two Gentlemen of Verona*", he composed "*Who is Sylvia?*"[7]

Early compositions (1810-1813)

Schubert's genius gradually began to manifest in his compositions. At the seminary, he devoted much of his time to compose chamber music, songs, piano pieces and, more ambitiously, liturgical choral works like, "*Salve Regna*", D. 27 and "*Kyrie*", D. 31.

In April, 1810, while still receiving lessons at the Stadtkonvikt, he wrote a grand fantasia for four hands, known by the name "*Corpse Fantasia*". This was followed in 1811 and 1813 by two less ambitious fantasias. In 1811, he composed two songs, "*Hagar's Klage*" (Hagar's Lament) and "*Der Vatermörder*" (The Parricide), several instrumental pieces, and the second fantasia for the pianoforte.

"*Hagar's Klage*" is particularly remarkable as being the first song of importance that Schubert composed. He wrote it on the 30 March 1811, at the age of fourteen; it amazed Salieri so much that he at once ordered further instruction in thoroughbass[8] to develop the rare gifts of the

---

[7] Newbould, Brian: "*Schubert: The Music and the Man*", University of California Press, Berkeley, Los Angeles, April 12, 1999.

[8] "*Thoroughbass*" (or "Figured bass"), is a kind of musical notation in which numerals and symbols (often accidentals) indicate intervals, chords, and non-chord tones that a musician playing piano, harpsichord, organ, lute (or other instruments capable of playing chords) play in relation to the bass note that these numbers and symbols appear above or below.

In the 20th and 21st century, thoroughbass is also sometimes used by classical musicians as a shorthand way of indicating chords when a composer is sketching out ideas for a new piece.

young genius. The teacher appointed for him, however, soon discovered that all such efforts were unnecessary as, the teacher reported to Salieri that the boy "*knows everything already*", and that "*he has been taught by God*". This report made Salieri even more interested in Schubert, so he himself undertook the young Schubert's guidance. And soon he was amazed at the luxuriant ease of Schubert's compositions. Schubert surprised Salieri by the complete partition of "*The Devil's Country Seat*". "*He can do everything*", Salieri exclaimed; "*he is a genius. He composes songs, masses, operas, quartets, — whatever you can think of.*"

In 1812, he composed the unfinished "*Octet for Winds*", D. 72 to commemorate the death of his mother; and in 1813 the he composed cantata[9] "*Werist gross*" (Who is big), D. 110 for male voices and orchestra to celebrate his father's birthday. During this period, he also composed for one of his brothers an andante[10] with variations, and thirty minuets[11] with trios. It surprised Anton Schmidt, a friend of Mozart's and a first-rate violinist, so much that he declared the boy who had written them would be a master such as few had ever been.

While he was still at school, he would participate in the family quartet practice, which generally took place on the Sunday afternoons. Schubert's father played the cello, Franz the viola, and two of his brothers the first and second violins. And most often the family would play the string quartets composed by him. In case of any mistake, the young Schubert would immediately note and would look seriously at the one to have goofed up, if he was one of his brothers; if it was his father, he would pass over the mistake once, but, on a repetition of it,

---

[9] A "*cantata*" is a vocal composition with an instrumental accompaniment, in several movements, typically with solos, chorus, and orchestra.

[10] The word '*andante*' is used to describe a relatively slow, moderately paced tune. An andante movement in a symphony is faster than 'adagio' but slower than '*allegro*'. Like so many musical words describing tempo, andante is Italian, a form of the verb *andare*, "to go."

[11] minutes

he would smile and say modestly, "*Father, there must be something wrong*" -- and that would be all.

In 1813, Schubert composed his maiden symphony, "*Symphony No. 1 in D major*", D. 82 when he was only 16. His first full-length opera, "*Des Teufels Lustschloss*" ("*The Devil's Palace of Desire*"), D. 84 was finished while he was still in Stadtkonvikt. [12][13]

---

[12] Schuster, M. Lincoln: "*The World's Great Letters*", Simon & Schuster Inc. New York City, New York, 1940.

[13] Crowest, Frederick J (Ed.): "*Schubert*" in "*The Master Musicians*" series published by J. M. Dent & Co., 29 & 30, Bedford Street, W.C., 1905.

Chapter 3
Schubert leaves Stadtkonvikt – joins his father's school as a teacher

In 1812, Schubert's voice broke; so he could not be retained as one of the singers in the Court Chapel. The Emperor gave him permission to remain in the school, but he was not inclined to continue, especially as it would have entailed a new examination.

Meanwhile, his mother had died in 1812. So, he decided to leave the school. Towards the end of 1813, he returned home to undergo teacher training programme at the St Anna Normal-hauptschule. In 1814, he entered his father's school as a teacher to teach little kids.

This was the beginning of the darkest period of his life. The clammy and shabby ambience of the school, the burden of his huge family frustrated him. He showed early signs of depression; it is also fairly certain that throughout his life Schubert suffered from *cyclothymia,* a mental illness that resulted in severe mood swings. It fluctuated between hypomania and depression; and his friends reported his having gone through frequent periods of dark despair and violent anger.[14] With burden on his heart, Schubert candidly admits:

> *"It's true that the children irritated me whenever I tried to create, and I lost the idea. Naturally I would beat them up."*

He started looking for some other job and sent petitions galore for sundry employment, but all in vain. He applied for military service but was rejected because of his short stature; so he had to remain content as a schoolmaster until 1818. In spite of his anxiety and mental agony, outwardly Schubert maintained his composure. He remained in the school job; alongside, he continued to receive lessons in composition

---

[14] Ho, Desiree: *"Franz Schubert's Illness: The Melancholy of an Autumnal Sunset",* Published in 'Interlude', 7 October 2011.

from Salieri for three more years and also composed prolifically. By 1814, he had written a number of piano pieces, and had produced string quartets, a symphony, and a three-act opera.

Chapter 4
The Musical journey: Early years (1814-1819)

Schubert is largely credited with creating the 'Lied', a type of German song composed by setting poetry to classical music, mostly composed in the 19th century Romantic period, typically for a solo voice with piano accompaniment. Boosted by a wealth of late 18th-century lyric poetry and the development of the piano, Schubert tapped the poetry of giants, like, Johann Wolfgang von Goethe, showing the world the possibility of representing their works in musical form.

During his lifetime, Schubert composed over 600 lieder (German songs), symphonies, operas, and a large body of chamber and piano music that adds up to over 1000 works during his career. This was prolific indeed for a man who lived for only 31 years.

"Gretchen am Spinnrade" ('Gretchen at the Spinning Wheel') (1814)

On October 19, 1814, Schubert wrote his first masterpiece *"Gretchen am Spinnrade"* ('Gretchen at the Spinning Wheel'), D. 118, Op. 2, a lied inspired by his reading of Goethe's *'Faust'*. In this musical piece, the piano is an integral element of the song; and it is a magical experience to listen to the accompaniment mimicking the revolving wheel, speeding up and slowing down in response to the text.

'Gretchen at the Spinning Wheel', Schubert, D. 118, Op. 2,

Besides '*Gretchen*', Schubert wrote five other Goethe songs during the same year. He was in love with Goethe's works. Before he died, he had set 57 poems by Goethe into music.

"*Der Erlkönig*" ('The Erl-King') *(1815)*

In 1815 alone, Schubert composed over 20,000 bars of music, more than half of which was for orchestra, including nine church works, half-a-dozen operas and operettas, several symphonies, and about 140 Lieder. Between May and December, he wrote four operas, namely, "*Der vierjährige Posten*" ('A Sentry for Four Years'), D.190, "*Fernando*" ('Fernando'), D. 220, "*Claudine von Villa Bella*" ('Claudine of Villa Bella'),D. 239,and "*Die Freunde von Salamanka*" ('The Friends of Salamanca'), D. 326. He also took a number of ballads from Goethe, Schiller, and Körner as well as songs from other popular poets of the day, and set them to music. These include "*Der Sanger*" ('*The Singer*'), D. 149, "An Mignon" ('At Mignon'), D. 161,"*Nurwer die SehnschustKennt*" ('Only who knows the Schehnschust'), D. 310, "*Kennst du dast Land*" ('Do you know that country?'), D. 321, "*Wersich der Einsamkeitergibt*" ('Who surrenders to loneliness'), D.

325 et al. He did it at an incredible speed; seven were composed on one day, and four on another.

Towards the end of 1815, Schubert composed his famous Lied "Der Erlkönig" ("The Erl-King"), D. 328, Op. 1, for solo voice and piano. The text of *Der Erlkönig* is set from a 1782 ballad by Goethe titled *"Die Fischerin"* (The Fisherwoman).

The poem that provides its text, like many of the supernatural tales that dominated literature in the Romantic era, has its roots in a Scandinavian folktale. It narrates the story of a boy riding home on horseback in his father's arms.

Johann Wolfgang von Goethe

As the poem unfolds, the son seems to see and hear creatures his father does not. The father tells the boy that his imagination is playing tricks on him. The boy grows increasingly terrified by what he hears from a supernatural being, the "Erlkönig" (Erl-King). His father seeks to explain to him that the things he thinks he sees and hears -- a wisp of fog, rustling leaves, shimmering willows -- are only the sights and sounds of nature on a dark and stormy night. Finally the child shrieks that he has been attacked. The father spurs on his horse to reach the

Hof (farm); but when he arrives home, he realizes that having been assailed by the evil supernatural being, the "Erlkönig", the child is dead.

Goethe's poem, translated into English by Edgar Alfred Browning, a British translator, author and civil servant (who later became Liberal Member of Parliament for Exeter (1868-1874)), which is reproduced below, depicts a conversation that includes the father, his child, and the evil Erl-King.[15]

Who rides there so late through the night dark and drear?

The father it is, with his infant so dear;

He holdeth the boy tightly clasp'd in his arm,

He holdeth him safely, he keepeth him warm.

"My son, wherefore seek'st thou thy face thus to hide?"

"Look, father, the Erl-King is close by our side!

Dost see not the Erl-King, with crown and with train?"

"My son, 'tis the mist rising over the plain."

"Oh, come, thou dear infant! oh come thou with me!

For many a game I will play there with thee;

On my strand, lovely flowers their blossoms unfold,

My mother shall grace thee with garments of gold."

"My father, my father, and dost thou not hear

The words that the Erl-King now breathes in mine ear?"

"Be calm, dearest child, 'tis thy fancy deceives;

'Tis the sad wind that sighs through the withering leaves."

"Wilt go, then, dear infant, wilt go with me there?

---

[15] *"The Poems of Goethe"* (1853), translated by Edgar Alfred Bowring, p. 99.

My daughters shall tend thee with sisterly care;
My daughters by night their glad festival keep,
They'll dance thee, and rock thee, and sing thee to sleep."
"My father, my father, and dost thou not see,
How the Erl-King his daughters has brought here for me?"
"My darling, my darling, I see it aright,
'Tis the aged grey willows deceiving thy sight."
"I love thee, I'm charm'd by thy beauty, dear boy!
And if thou'rt unwilling, then force I'll employ."
"My father, my father, he seizes me fast,
For sorely the Erl-King has hurt me at last."
The father now gallops, with terror half wild,
He grasps in his arms the poor shuddering child;
He reaches his courtyard with toil and with dread, –
The child in his arms finds he motionless, dead.

Schubert deftly underscores the action described in the poem by carefully crafting music that drops the listener in the midst of things. He heightens its horror by his creative genius. "Although only one singer is involved, Schubert gives each of the song's four personalities—narrator, father, boy, and Erl-King—a characteristic way of singing." Each time the boy speaks, his growing hysteria is signaled by his rising vocal pitch, whereas the father's voice, though lower in pitch, is steady and even. "The Erl-King's voice, by contrast, is initially sweetly beguiling, but, as he loses his patience with the boy, it takes on an angry, menacing edge."

Schubert revised "*Der Erlkönig*" three times before publishing the final version in 1821. The same year his friend Vogl sang it at a public concert in an opera-house; and it at once became a hot favourite of all music lovers and made Schubert a popular name in the Vienna music circle. *"Der Erlkönig"* sold an unheard of more than 800 copies.

Schubert once performed *"Der Erlkönig"* on a comb and tissue paper.

"String Quartet No. 11 in E major" (1816)

Schubert's creative spree continued in 1816, when he was barely 19. Songs of this period include "Gesänge des Harfners" ('Harper's Songs')[16] from Goethe's novel *"Wilhelm Meisters Lehrjahren"* ('Wilhelm Meister's Apprenticeship'), *"Der Wanderer"* ('The hiker'), D. 489, Op. 4, No. 1 and *"Ganymed"* ('The Cup bearer of God'), D. 544, Op. 19, No. 3. This apart, he also composed two symphonies, namely, *"Symphony No. 4 in C minor"* ('Tragic'), D 417, and the popular *"Symphony No. 5 in B-flat major"*, D. 485, and a Mass in C major.

Schubert began composing string quartets[17] when he was thirteen, initially to play with his family. His first *"String Quartet No. 1"*, D. 18, in 'mixed keys', was written in 1810 and it was followed by 14 more string quartets, with the last coming in 1826, two years before his early death. The quartet is original-sounding and has some rather unusual characteristics not found elsewhere. It makes no technical demands of the players and though simple, it is still effective, both good to play and to hear.

---

[16] 'Harper's Songs', namely, *"Werniesien Brotmitm Tranen aß"* ('He who never eats bread with tears'), *"An die Turen will ich Schleichen"* ('I want to sneak to the doors'), D. 478 et al.

[17] A *'quartet'* is an ensemble of four singers or instrumental performers; or a musical composition for four voices or instruments. In Classical music, the most important combination of four instruments in 'chamber music'** is the string quartet. String quartets most often consist of two violins, a viola, and a cello.

"Chamber music" is a form of classical music composed for a small group of instruments—traditionally a group that could fit in a palace chamber or a large room. In a broad sense, it includes any art music that is performed by a small number of performers, with one performer to a part (in contrast to orchestral music, in which each string part is played by a number of performers). However, by convention, it usually does not include solo instrument performances.

The quartets composed by Schubert in his initial years are, however, not considered amongst his major works; but it took him not much time to mature. He was certainly familiar with many of the quartets of the earlier virtuosi, like, Haydn, Mozart, Rossini, and Beethoven; and with his amazingly unconventional approach befitting a genius he soon began chartering new territories. By the time he was sixteen, he composed "*String Quartet No. 4 in C Major*", D. 46 that bears the signature of a true master-in-the-making.

In 1816, Schubert composed his famous "*String Quartet No. 11 in E major*", D. 353; it was posthumously published as Op. 125 No. 2.

Schubert: Rejected for the post of a music teacher in Laibach

By now, Schubert was tired of his job as a school teacher in a kindergarten school. He was desperately looking for another job.

In the spring of 1816, Schubert sent a petition to the Royal Civic Guard headquarters in Vienna begging to be considered for the vacant post of a music teacher in Laibach, about 300 miles away from Vienna. The salary was small — 500 florins Viennese, but Schubert needed the job badly and applied with great hope and expectation. In his application letter, he wrote "*he has acquired such knowledge and skill in all branches of composition, in the practice of the organ and the violin as well as in singing that, as the enclosed certificates will show, of all candidates for the post, he will be found to be the best qualified.*"; he ended his petition declaring that "*in the event of a favourable answer he solemnly promises to make the best possible use of his power so as to give complete satisfaction.*"

As his reference, Schubert gave the name of his teacher, Salieri, the famous musician of the day, who was not only his mentor -- he was one who always considered Schubert a genius. Despite his strong credentials, Schubert did not get the job for which he petitioned so humbly. Salieri failed to live up to his expectations; he recommended another pupil for the job. Schubert was disappointed, but he maintained his poise and plunged himself entirely into music and produced several masterpieces.

"Die Forelle" ('The Trout') *((1817)*

In 1817, Schubert set to music the lyrics of the lied *"Die Forelle"*('The Trout') , D. 550,Op. 32, written in early 1817 by German poet Christian Friedrich Daniel Schubert;

The full poem tells the story of a trout being caught by a fisherman, but in its final stanza, there is an apparent moral warning to young women to guard against young men. When Schubert set the poem to music, he removed the last verse, which contained the moral warning, changing the song's focus.

The song became extremely popular with the contemporary audience; and it led to Schubert being commissioned to write a piece of chamber music based on the song. This resulted in the famous *"Trout"* quintet, D. 667, Op. 114 that he composed in 1819in which a set of variations of "*Die Forelle*" is present in the fourth movement.

The same year, Schubert began his masterly series of piano sonatas, six of which were composed at his closest friend Schober's home; the finest being *"Piano Sonata in E-flat major"*, D. 568, Op.122and *"Piano Sonata in B major"*, D. 575 (posthumously published as Op. 147). The year 1817 is also marked by the composition of the two "overtures in the Italian style".

Schubert joins his father as a teacher in a new school, albeit reluctantly

In late 1817 Schubert's father gained a new position at a school in Rossau, not far from Lichtental. Schubert reluctantly joined his father at his new place of work. In 1818 spring, he produced only one major work, the *"Symphony No. 6 in C Major"*, D. 589, nicknamed '*Little C Major*' to distinguish it from his later Ninth Symphony, in the same key, which is known as the "*Great C major*". In the meantime, his reputation was growing, and he earned some favourable reviews for his compositions.

Schubert's unhappy years as a school teacher ended in the summer of 1818; he left the school job to pursue music full-time. His decision was sparked by a gradually growing welcome audience for his music, and also in part by the first public performance of one of his works, the "*Italian Overture in C Major*", D. 591, on March 1, 1818, in Vienna.

Summer of 1818: Schubert becomes private music teacher of Marie & Caroline

In June, Schubert left the city to take up the post of a private music teacher to the two daughters of Count Johann Karl Esterhazy, for the summer months, in the family's summer residence at Zseliz, Hungary (now, in Slovakia).The pay was relatively good, though he was not treated so respectably, being housed with gardeners and other menials of the palace. The burden of teaching piano and singing to the two daughters, Marie and Caroline, was however relatively light, allowing him time to compose happily. Letters to his friends during this period show him in exuberant spirits, and the summer months were marked by a fresh creative outburst.

During this period, Schubert wrote some of his loveliest and most enduring music, like, "*Marche Militairein D. major*" ('Military marches'), D. 733, op. 51 for Marie and Caroline, for instructional purposes, in addition to other piano duets. The piano duets "*Variations on a French Song in E minor*", D. 624, Op. 10 sets of dances, songs, and the "*Deutsche Trauermesse*" ('German Requiem'), D. 621, were also completed. On his return to Vienna, he took up residence with his friend and poet Johann Mayrhofer.

Schubert is said to have had a hopeless passion and unrequited love towards his pupil Countess Caroline, but the difference in their social and economic status made anything more than a platonic romance impossible

"Die Zwillingsbrüder" ('The Twin Brothers') *(1819)*

During 1819 winter, Schubert composed "*Die Zwillingsbrüder*", D. 647 ('The Twin Brothers'), a one act Singspiel[18],on a libretto ('text') by Georg Ernst von Hofmann, an Austrian occasional poet, which was performed in June 1820 and met with some success. In June 1819 Schubert and his team-singer, Vogl, set off for a holiday tour in the singer's native district in upper Austria. Schubert was charmed by the beauty of the countryside and was touched by the warm reception given everywhere to his music. At Steyr, he composed the first of his widely known instrumental compositions, the *"Piano Sonata in A Major"*, D. 664, and the celebrated *"Trout"* quintet.

The 'Trout' Quintet (1819)

Schubert composed the famous *"Trout"* quintet, D. 667 in 1819; but it was published a decade later in 1829, only after his death.

The piece is known as the *'Trout'* because the fourth movement is a set of variations on his earlier lied *"Die Forelle"* ".The *"Trout"* was written for Sylvester Paumgartner, a wealthy music patron and amateur cellist of Steyr in Upper Austria, who suggested that Schubert include a set of variations on the lied.

The *'Trout* is a leisurely work for piano and strings characterized by lower structural coherence especially, in its outer movements and the Andante.

The quintet forms the basis of Christopher Nupen's 1969 film *"The Trout"*, performed, amongst others, by Zubin Mehta at Queen Elizabeth Hall in London. [19][20]

----

[18] A *"Singspiel"*(literally 'sing-play')is a form of German-language music drama, now regarded as a genre of opera. Singspiel plots are generally comic or romantic in nature, and frequently include elements of magic, fantastical creatures, and comically exaggerated characterizations of good and evil.

[19] Schwarm, Betsy: *"Erlkönig, Song by Schubert"*, Encyclopedia Britannica.

[20] Bodley, Lorraine Byrne. *"Schubert's Goethe Settings"*, published by Ashgate, 2003.

Chapter 5
Schubert's friends: Friends in need

Schubert grew up in the shadow of fear. With the rise of Napoleon Bonaparte in the mid-1790s and a large contingent of the French army advancing on Vienna, public morale was plummeting. In a desperate bid to raise flagging spirits, Vienna turned to poets and composers for some respite.

Schubert's Vienna was a dangerous place to speak one's mind. One had, therefore, to choose one's friends carefully. And Schubert, on the whole, chose well. He developed a network of friends that included poets, singers, and musicians, who stood by him like a rock in his hours of need and helped preserve and promote his work after his death.

Schubert was natural at making friends, and also at keeping the relationship. Several friendships formed at the Seminary lasted throughout his life. Schubert's circle of friends, bound together by a passion for poetry and music, includes some of the finest artists of the 19th century. Below are some of Schubert's friends and acquaintances who stood by him in hours of crisis and played an important role in his life.

Franz von Schober

In 1815, he met Franz von Schober, born in Sweden and whose father had emigrated, but who returned to Germany on his father's death and started living in Vienna. Scion of an affluent family, Schober was fascinated by some of Schubert's songs and desired to meet him. Soon he became an ardent admirer of the composer. Ever since he met him, he felt Schubert was wasting his time in teaching the kids in an elementary school; so he constantly tried to persuade him to get rid of the drudgery of his school job. Once, late in 1815, Schober went to the schoolhouse where Schubert was teaching; there he found him in front of a class with his manuscripts piled about him– an uninterested listener, with a desire to break free from his duties.

Franz von Schober

Charismatic and sophisticated, Schober was in many ways the most prominent amongst Schubert's friends. Tall, handsome, and articulate, he was in many respects Schubert's polar opposite. Oozing charisma, he quite overwhelmed the diminutive, tongue-tied Schubert, who quickly became his adoring admirer. And he was hardly alone. Schubert's friend and former schoolmate Eduard von Bauernfeld was almost equally entranced: *"Schober surpasses us all in mind, and still more so in speech!"*

Eduard von Bauernfeld

Schober was certainly Schubert's closest and the most influential friend; he helped Schubert in promoting his music and in establishing useful opportunities and contacts for him in the early part of his career. He also provided him with lodging for extended periods

After Schubert had set some of Goethe's poems to music -- *"Gretchen at the Spinning Wheel"* et al. – Schober and a few other friends of Schubert tried to interest Goethe in the songs. In April 1816 they sent a volume of 16 settings to the poet, but to no effect.

The Hüttenbrenner brothers: Anselm and Joseph Hüttenbrenner

In 1815, the same year he met Schober, Schubert also developed a friendship with Ansclm Hüttenbrenner, a lawyer and composer, and a pupil of Salieri. He also became a friend of Anslelm's brother Josef, an amateur musician, who played a major role in promoting his music.

Anselm Hüttenbrenner

Josef was an ardent admirer of Schubert's genius; and as a genuine well-wisher, he tirelessly attempted to bring some semblance of order to Schubert's chaotic professional life. Josef's love for Schubert was almost idolatry; so effusive was it that it at times irritated the bohemian composer. So, despite Josef's passionate adoration and enthusiasm for his music, he would at times say ironically: "*That one (Josef) is pleased with everything I do*".

Josef Hüttenbrenner

Schubert was, however, appreciative of Josef's untiring services in arranging his symphonies for the piano, in attending to his works being engraved, and in corresponding with his publishers.

Schubert wrote a beautiful set of variations on a theme by Anselm Hüttenbrenner -- known as the "*Hüttenbrenner variations*", D. 567.

Johann Mayrhofer

Towards the end of 1816, Schober invited Schubert to stay with him in the home of his widowed mother in Vienna. By then, on persistent persuasion by Schober, Schubert had decided not to resume his old teaching job at his father's school; he, therefore, accepted the proposal and started living with him. After some time, on the arrival of a brother of his host, it became necessary for Schubert to move. So he moved to reside with his poet friend Johann Mayrhofer, many of whose verses he had set to music.

Johann Mayrhofer

Schober and Mayrhofer were amongst his closest friends. In early 1817, Schober introduced him to Johann Michael Vogl, a prominent Austrian baritone, considerably older than Schubert, who had long been engaged in the Viennese opera. The friendship between Schubert and Vogl began in 1817, and it exerted a beneficial influence on the young composer. Soon the two formed a sensational duo that would be remembered in the history of music for a long time to come.

Schubert teams up with Vogl

Born on August 10, 1768, Vogl came to Vienna in 1786 to study, and later to practice law. In 1795 he debuted at the Wiener Hofoper ('Vienna State Opera') and quickly attracted a following for both his acting capability and mellifluous voice. Soon Vogl became a celebrated singer in the musical circle in Vienna. Two years later, in 1797, Franz Schubert, with whom he was to form a historic musical partnership, was born in Vienna.

In 1813, Schubert attended a performance of Gluck's "*Iphigenie en Tauride*" ('Iphigenie en Tauride') in which Vogl sang the lead role. Vogl was a sensation at that time. Schubert never forgot the experience and was determined to write to him; he became his ardent admirer.

The following year, Vogl sang the role of Pizarro at the premiere of the final version of Beethoven's *"Fidelio"*. It is said that the 17-year-old Schubert actually sold his schoolbooks in order to afford a ticket.

Johann Michael Vogl

As a passionate admirer of Vogl, Schubert longed to have him as the singer for the songs he composed. But initially Vogl shunned his acquaintance. Schober had spoken to Vogl several times about Schubert, but without effect. At last one fine morning in 1817, he agreed to pay a visit to the young composer and *"was received by him with rather awkward bows and scrapes and disconnected words, and hummed over one or two songs"*. The first one itself seemed to him *"pretty and melodious"*; and as he heard more, he became completely beholden to the young genius. While leaving, he tapped Schubert on the shoulder and said, "*There is something in you, but you are too little of an actor, too little of a charlatan; you squander your good thoughts instead of beating them out fine*".

Vogl was simply bowled over by Schubert's music. The songs grew upon him more and more. It was now his turn to be an ardent admirer of the budding composer, barely out of his teens, who was about 30 years younger than him. To others, he spoke warmly and enthusiastically of Schubert. Before long he came to Schubert uninvited to study his compositions and soon he communicated to others the raptures they awoke in him.

And there was looking back thereafter. It took the duo no time to form a musical pair -- and the rest is history. Soon Vogl's singing of Schubert's songs became the rage of the Viennese drawing rooms.

Schubert wrote many of his songs with Vogl in mind. One of their early successes was an 1821 performance of '*Der Erlkönig*'. Together they created history. Rarely in the music world has a composer and a singer duo been musically so productive.

A cartoon showing Franz Schubert and his singer friend Vogl

Vogl not only sang the songs composed by Schubert, but he also guided his choice as to the poems which he was to set to music; he would recite them beforehand to Schubert with great power of expression so that the music might do full justice to the thought of the poet. Schubert generally came to Vogl's lodging in the morning, and either composed there or went through new songs with him. Schubert attached much importance to Vogl's judgement, and often accepted his corrections.

It was Vogl who first made Schubert known to the world of art. In fine, he acted as his guide and adviser, and did all in his power to improve Schubert's circumstances. Perhaps he acted too much as a protector, which is partly explained by his being about thirty years older than his companion. In 1823 Schubert wrote in a letter: "*He is taken up with my songs almost exclusively. He writes out the voice-part himself and, so to speak, lives on it*".

Vogl continued to sing Schubert's music even after his friend's death in 1828, famously singing a complete performance of "*Winterreise*" accompanied by the pianist Emanuel Mikschik shortly before his own death on the twelfth anniversary of the death of his friend. Vogl sang in the Viennese opera for twenty-eight years; his judgment of Schubert's songs is rather singular. In the words of Vogl:

> "*Nothing has shown the want of an efficient school of singing so clearly as Schubert's songs. Otherwise, what an extraordinary and universal effect wherever the German language penetrates would have been produced by these truly divine inspirations, these utterance of a musical clairvoyance...How many would have understood for the first time the meaning of the words, language, poetry in notes, words in harmonies, thoughts clothed in music? They would have learnt how the finest poem of our greatest poets can be elevated, or even surpassed when translated into such musical language.*"

Josef von Gahy

Among Schubert's other musical friends was a civil servant named Gahy, a pianist with whom he played duets. Gahy was selected by Schubert to play compositions for four hands with him on the piano, his own works and the symphonies of Beethoven. The purity and expressiveness of Gahy's play, and the quickness with which he read music at sight were the points that endeared him to the composer.

Schubertiades

By the early 1820s, Schubert became part of a close-knit circle of friends, musicians and artists. This group held frequent informal social gatherings at private homes to celebrate Schubert's music. Such events came to be known as *"Schubertiades"*, and were often sponsored by aristocrats, high-ranking civil servants and wealthy men of business, who sought release from the boredom of their routine life. A typical Schubertiade would generally begin with the performance of Schubert songs, often new ones and usually accompanied by the composer himself with Vogl on the piano, after which he and his friends would play piano duets or join together in lively vocal quartets. In addition to Schubert's music, *Schubertiades* often also featured poetry readings, dancing, and other sociable pastimes.

A Glimpse of a Schubertiade

The *Schubertiades* became very popular and were sometimes held in places outside Vienna. Schubert's popularity soon expanded far and wide and he became a craze amongst the young music lovers and a well-known name in the Vienna music circle.

Schubert at the pianoforte during a Schubertiade

Unfortunately, about the same time, Schubert and a few of his close circle of friends had a bitter experience that dealt a death blow to their friendship. A friend of Schubert from his Seminary days, Johann Senn, was a passionate supporter of Tyrolese independence. After the police raid on his residence in March 1820, Schubert, though innocent, was also arrested along with four of his friends by the Austrian secret police. Senn was imprisoned for fourteen months without charges being brought against him, and then permanently forbidden to enter Vienna. The other four, including Schubert, were severely reprimanded, on the charge of protesting against the arresting police officials and using abusive language. After this unfortunate occurrence, Schubert never saw Senn again in his life. The incident apparently also played a role in his falling out with his friend, Mayrhofer, with whom he was living at that time. [21][22][23]

---

[21] Flower, Newman: *"Franz Schubert - The Man And His Circle"*, Tudor Publishing Co., New York, December, 1935.

[22] Tomes, Susan: *"Out of Silence: A Pianist's Yearbook"*, The Boydell Press, Woodbridge, 2010, p. 147.

[23] Gibbs, Christopher H.: *"The Life of Schubert"*, Cambridge University Press, March 2015.

Johann Chrysostomus Senn

Chapter 6
The Musical Journey: The Middle years (1820-1824)

The close of 1819 saw him engrossed in composing songs to poems by his friend Mayrhofer and by Goethe, who inspired his masterly dramatic art song *'Prometheus'*, D. 674.

On June 14, 1820, *"Die Zwillingsbrüder"* ('The Twin Brothers'), D.647, a one-act singspiel (a form of German drama, now regarded as a genre of opera) based on a libretto by Georg Ernst von Hofmann, was performed with moderate success at the Kärntnertortheater in Vienna. It was followed by the performance of incidental music for the play *"Die Zauberharfe"* ('The Magic Harp'),D. 644,a melodrama in three acts based on a text by Georg von Hofmann, debuted in August of the same year. The lovely, melodious overture became famous as the *'Rosamunde'* overture.

In December, 1820, he began the choral setting of Goethe's *"Gesang der Geisterüber den Wassern"* ('Song of the Spirits over the Water'), D. 714, and completed it in February 1821. Within the same month in 1820, Schubert composed his famous *"Quartettsatz in C minor"*. Soon it became a trendsetter and sparked a wave of string quartets far and wide in Vienna and outside; and also dominated the music scene for several years to come.

Quartettsatz in C-moll (Quartet Movement in C minor) *(1820)*

Schubert began work on the *"Quartettsatz in C-moll"*, D. 703 ('Quartet Movement in C minor'), in early December 1820, shortly after a "Schubertiade" was held at the home of Austrian Jurist, writer and educator Ignaz von Sonnleithner on December 1, 1820.Before the month was over, he composed the *"Quartettsatz"*. It was his first attempt at writing a string quartet since completing the *"String Quartet*

No. 11 in E major", D 353 in 1816; but he abruptly abandoned the work and never completed. It was listed as his *"String Quartet No. 12"* on publication.

Ignaz von Sonnleithner

The 'unfinished' quartet is regarded as an outstanding creative work of Schubert's mature phase of composition. Four years after the "*Quartettsatz*", Schubert returned to the genre to write the *Rosamunde Quartet*, D 804, which was followed by the "*Death and the Maiden*" Quartet D 810 and the *"Fifteenth Quartet"*, D 887.

There has been much speculation on why Schubert left the composition incomplete. One view presented by Bernard Shore, the author of *"Sixteen Symphonies"*, is that Schubert put it aside to pursue another musical idea and later lost track of it. Others feel he might have abandoned it as it "*...did not yet represent the great leap forward he was striving for.*"

Following Schubert's death, the manuscript score came to be owned by the famous German composer and pianist, Johannes Brahms. At his instance, it was performed on March 1, 1867, in Vienna, and the score, edited by Brahms, was published later in 1870.

Schubert: Count Dietrichstein recognizes his genius

Little did Napoleon realize, when releasing Count Moritz Dietrichstein from a French prison in 1800, that the Austrian nobleman would one day be responsible for the education of his son, Napoleon II. A musical connoisseur, Dietrichstein became the child's governor after Napoleon's 1815 defeat and remained in that capacity until the boy's death in 1832.

Dietrichstein was an able composer. He studied with the Abbé Stadler and composed vocal music, both sacred and secular, as well as a number of dances. In 1811, he published 16 settings of Goethe's poems to music, dedicating them to the poet, who praised their "charm" and "original character." Dietrichstein also organized concerts for Beethoven, whom he revered.

In 1819 Dietrichstein was appointed the musical director of the imperial court. In 1821 he also became director of the court theatres.

Count Dietrichstein was impressed with Schubert's genius. At the beginning of 1821, he sent Schubert a testimonial endorsed by him and also signed by Salieri, the imperial Kapellmeister, and Weigl, the Deputy Kapellmeister of the court, to help him get a job. The testimonial described Schubert as a composer with great promise and that in all fairness an opportunity should be given him to develop his genius for the benefit of art and music. Weigl and Salieri also said pretty much the same highlighting the young master's brilliance in composition and his mastery of theoretical and practical harmony.

The successful *"Der Erlkönig"* ('The Erl-King'), D. 328, Op. 1 composed by Schubert was published the same year. Schubert dedicated it to Count Dietrichstein -- ostensibly as a token of gratitude for his kindness. The dedication helped Schubert to gain the attention of the publishers of the day who realized that he was not a man to be neglected, particularly when "Erl King" turned to be a roaring success.

Soon, however, the publishers also realized that Schubert, though a musical genius, was one without any business sense and that he can easily be exploited. In 1821, a number of Schubert's works, including the popular lied *"Der Erlkönig"* had been published. The pecuniary result of his publications of that year was quite good; 2000 guldens were realised, and of the *"Der Erlkönig"* alone more than 800 copies were sold. If Schubert had been prudent to keep his work in his own possession, it would have greatly benefitted him and he would soon have been out of financial distress. But instead, being pressed by the want of money, he sold twelve songs to his Austrian publisher Anton Diabelli for 800 florins, by one of which alone (*'The Wanderer'*), the publisher made 36,000 florins over the period of copyright. And this was not the only one; Schubert entered into some more financially unwise arrangement with the same firm for his future publications.

Anton Diabelli

The publishers, as is their wont, took great advantage of Schubert's lack of financial prudence. Even when he became well known, he sold his famous masterpiece –the song cycle *"Winterreise"* -- to his publisher for a mere twenty cents apiece.

"Der Tod und das Madchen" ('Death and the Maiden') *[1821]*

During 1821 and the three following years, Schubert wrote almost all his dance music -- about seventy-nine waltzes and twenty- eight ecossaises (a type of Scottish country dance– that was popular in France and Great Britain at the end of the 18th century and at the beginning of the 19th).. About the same time, he was commissioned to write two additional pieces for Herold's Opera " *Les Clochettes*" ('The Bells'). He gladly accepted the offer as he was desirous of employing himself on dramatic music, wrote a tenor aria and a comic duet.

In November 1821, *"Der Tod und das Mädchen"* ("Death and the Maiden"), a beautiful lied composed by Schubert in February 1817, was published by Cappi and Diabelli in Vienna. The text is derived from a poem written by German poet Matthias Claudius. The song is set for voice and piano. The piece begins with an introduction in D minor and dwells on the musical theme of Death.

Schubert's popularity grows, but success still remains elusive

Schubert's fortunes began to change in 1821, when, with the help of some friends, he began offering his songs in concert parties in social gatherings in the city. Money started coming his way. Schubert's harmonious songs and dances soon became very popular not only in Vienna but outside too.

With his growing musical fame, Schubert started receiving many invitations; but being timid and indifferent, he was not very comfortable in upper crust social gatherings. So the number of elite families with whom he developed intimacy was comparatively small. While Beethoven, who lived in the same city, was recognised almost exclusively in aristocratic circles, Schubert, on the contrary, mingled more with the middle classes and had many friends of various ranks and positions. With these friends he passed a gala time, frequented cafes and gardens, participated in many concert parties (*'Schubertiades'*) in the homes of wealthy residents across the city and outside Vienna; he also made many a long excursion into the country. It was a happy time for Schubert.

One of these excursions was to the *Schloss Ochsenburg* ('Castle Ochsenburg'), and here Schubert passed the autumn months of the year 1821 with his friend Schober writing the text of an opera, while he set it to music. The opera in question – "*Alfonso and Estrella*", D 732, a musical play in three acts with music composed by Schubert, and libretto by his friend Schober --- is one of his masterpieces.

Alfonso und Estrella (1822)

Between September 1821 and February 1822, Schubert wrote the vocal numbers of "*Alfonso und Estrella*". The theme of the opera is the love between Alfonso, son of Froila, the deposed King of Leon, and Estrella; the daughter of Mauregato, the usurper of Froila's throne. Alfonso, in exile with his father Froila, and living in an idyllic valley, is determined to restore the lost kingdom from Mauregato.

At the court of Leon, Adolfo, an ambitious general, is the villain of the piece; he desires to have Estrella. But Mauregato makes a precondition that only the man who has the "*Chain of Eurich*" may marry Estrella. An angry Adolfo plans a coup against Mauregato. Meanwhile, during a hunting expedition, Alfonso meets Estrella, estranged from her associates, and they fall in love unaware of the identity of each other. Alfonso gives Estrella a necklace he has always carried and guides her on a safe path home.

Back at court, Estrella narrates her story. Mauregato recognizes the necklace as the "*Chain of Eurich*". But before he can tell her its meaning, Adolfo stages a coup and captures Estrella as a prisoner. She is ultimately rescued by Alfonso, who overpowers Adolfo. In the changed circumstances, a repentant Mauregato, as a token of gratitude, restores Froila to his throne. Froila, in turn, gives it to his son Alfonso, as both the fathers bless the marriage of their children.

Unfortunately for Schubert, the orchestral version of the opera was not staged in Schubert's lifetime. Opera houses in Vienna, Berlin, Dresden, and Graz refused to try it, afraid to take a chance on a young composer like Schubert, whose music was not considered traditional.

Years after Schubert's death, the opera received its premiere performance in Weimer on 24 June 1854, conducted by Franz Liszt. Subsequent productions in the 1880s were in Karlsruhe, Vienna, and Berlin. The first UK stage premiere was at Reading University Opera on 22 February 1977; but the opera never received a complete, uncut performance.

When Liszt produced "*Alfonso und Estrella*" at Weimar in 1854, it had only a modest success, and Liszt himself confessed that its performance must be regarded merely as *ein Act der Pietat* ['an act of piety'] and an execution of historic justice. He called attention to the fact that Schubert, who in his songs contributed such picturesque and expressive accompaniments, should in this opera have assigned to the instruments such a subordinate role that it seemed little more than a pianoforte accompaniment arranged for the orchestra. At the same time, as Liszt very properly adds, Schubert influenced the progress of opera indirectly, by showing in his songs how closely poetry can be wedded to music, and that it can be emotionally intensified by its impassioned accents. Nor must one overlook the fact that there are in these sort of Schubert operas not a few melodies, beautiful as such, which we can enjoy at home or in the concert hall. These melodies are too lyrical in style to save the operas.

"*Alfonso und Estrella*" has been criticized for its lack of dramatic action and pacing, though it is acknowledged that Schubert displays his usual genius in composing its music. In the words of a critic: " *in this composition, Schubert's great operatic asset, aside from his incredible gift for melody, is the ability to take cues from a word, a thought or a verbal description and translate them into musical accompaniment*"

The refusal of the opera house owners to stage "*Alfonso und Estrella*" depressed him. It seemed to him his fate was sealed. But undeterred by his frustration and failure, Schubert continued with his indomitable creative spirit.

"Mein Traum" ("My Dream") *(1822)*

In July 1822, while holidaying with Schober and other friends at Atzenbrugg, a municipality in the district of Tulln in Lower Austria, Schubert wrote a short prose titled *"Mein Traum"* ("My Dream"). It is an interesting tale of exile and homecoming and depicts a conflict between a music-loving youth and his father. It offers new insights into the composer's life and personality as it reveals the underlying anxiety, insecurity, and loneliness of the young genius. It brings to the fore many of his innate feelings as Schubert recounts a dream of being driven out of his father's house and forced to wander in foreign lands.

Ten years after Schubert's death, his brother, Ferdinand, gave the original manuscript of "Mein Traum" to Robert Schumann, who published it in the February 5, 1839, issue of his journal, the "Neue Zeitschrift für Musik" ('New Journal for Music').

This apart, in the very same year, Schubert composed the beautiful four-movement *"Fantasie in C major"*– popularly known as the *"Wanderer Fantasy"*--for solo piano, and his timeless masterpiece – the two-movement *"Unfinished Symphony"* in B minor.

Schubert's 'Unfinished' Symphony': "Symphony No. 8 in B minor" (1822)

In October 1822, Schubert started his "Symphony No. 8 in B minor", D. 759 ((sometimes renumbered as Symphony No. 7,[24] in accordance with the revised Deutsch catalogue and the *Neue Schubert-Ausgabe*,[25] commonly known as the *"Unfinished Symphony"*, but left with only two movements. And though he lived for another six years, he never cared to complete the work. It came to light more than three decades

---

[24] *"Franz Schubert, Complete Symphonies, Robert Cummings"*. Bamberg Symphony, Jonathan Nott, Tudor 7141 Hybrid Multichannel SACD

[25] *"D-Verz.: 759, Titel: Sinfonie Nr.7 "*. Neue Schubert-Ausgabe, Schubert-database.

after his death. A *scherzo*,[26] nearly completed in piano score but with only two pages orchestrated, also survives.

Schubert wrote the *"Unfinished Symphony"* for the *Musikverein of Graz* ('Graz Musical Society') when they granted him an honorary membership. He completed two movements, thereafter confined it to his drawer and left it unperformed. Later he gave the manuscript to his good friend Anselm Hüttenbrenner Anselm was part of the society and Schubert's closest link to it, which is why he was the one to receive the score. But oddly enough, Anselm did not show it to the society at that time nor did he ever reveal to anyone that he had this wonderful new piece.

The 'Unfinished' Symphony': Composed in 1822, premiered in 1865—37 years after his death

Six years after the composition of the *"Unfinished Symphony"*, in November 1828 Schubert died. Anselm kept it a secret for another 37 years. Finally in 1865, when he was 76 years old and approaching death (he died three years later), he showed it to the Viennese conductor Johann von Herbeck. It was only then the *"Unfinished Symphony"* was performed for the first time at a concert given by the *Society of Music Friends in Vienna*, under Herbeck, on December 7, 1865. At the performance, Schubert's *Symphony No. 3* in D major was added as the finale, though the style did not match The Unfinished Symphony. Nevertheless, the audience loved it; but this was not adhered to subsequently. As a matter of fact, the two finished movements as such form a complete whole. The mystery surrounding the composition of the symphony is one of the most intriguing puzzles in the entire realm of music.

---

[26] A '*scherzo*', in western classical music, is a short composition – sometimes a movement from a larger work such as a symphony or a sonata. The precise definition has varied over the years, but scherzo often refers to a movement that replaces the minuet as the third movement in a four-movement work, such as a symphony, sonata, or string quartet

Schubert's 'Unfinished Symphony' - at Macomb Center for the Performing Arts - by Detroit Symphony Orchestra

The performance captivated the audience; the world saw what Schubert was capable of! This is the most romantic of all Schubert's symphonies. A new world of sound is created here, harmony, finely graded according to the individual colour of each instrument, and melody shaded to a minute degree Since then the *"Unfinished Symphony"* has been considered one of the finest symphonies ever composed. The score of the two movements was published in 1867.

Schubert began his unfinished symphony in this house

British writer, music journalist Tom Service described the '*Unfinished Symphony*' as *"one of the greatest, and strangest, of the genre"*. The Austrian cellist, viol player, and conductor Nikolaus Harnoncourt remarked that the '*Unfinished Symphony*' has all the strangeness, surprise, and shock of a *"stone from the moon"*.

The often brutal music critic, Eduard Hanslick, attended the 1865 premiere of the symphony and wrote afterwards:

> *"When, after a few introductory bars, clarinet and oboe sound una voce[27] a sweet melody on top of the quiet murmuring of the strings, any child knows the composer and a half-suppressed exclamation "Schubert" runs hummingly through the hall. He has hardly entered, but it is as if you knew his steps, his very way of opening the door... The whole movement is a sweet stream of melodies, in spite of its vigor and geniality so crystal-clear that you can see every pebble on the bottom. And everywhere the same warmth, the same golden sunshine that makes buds grow!"*

Hanslick believed it to be Schubert's most beautiful composition. [28]

What makes a Symphony "unfinished"?

A classical symphony is usually made up of four movements. With the first and last movements being written in the same key, known as the "home key." In contrast, Schubert's "*Unfinished Symphony*" has only two complete full movements, with an incomplete third movement; the rest of the scherzo was found in Schubert's papers after his death.

---

[27] (i) The *oboe* is a type of double-reed woodwind instrument. Oboes are usually made of wood, but may also be made of synthetic materials, such as plastic, resin, or hybrid composites. It has a warm, reedy, almost squawking sound. The pitch of the oboe is easily "lipped" higher or lower by the player, and a well-trained oboist is able to play long passages and long notes in a single breath due to the nature of the instrument.

(ii) Una voce: with one voice

[28] "Franz Schubert: The Last Classical Composer and his Symphony No. 8 "Unfinished"", The Classical Difference. https://www.classicaldifference.com/schubert/

However, that portion was not fully scored, meaning he had only written it for piano, and not for orchestra.

The first movement of *"The Unfinished symphony"* is written in B minor and the second movement is written in E major, and the incomplete third movement returns to B minor. Since the third movement returned to B minor it indicates that Schubert was not finished and intended to follow the classical format by returning to the home key.[29][30]

But why did Schubert leave the symphony "unfinished"?

According to Schubert's biographer George R. Marek, the composer came to learn of his syphilis infection in late 1823; and perhaps it prompted him to abandon the composition of *"Unfinished Symphony"*. But Schubert lived for another six years and composed several other pieces. Why therefore he never returned to the '*Unfinished Symphony*' remains a mystery.

Many music historians and scholars are of the view the composition is complete in its two-movement form, and indeed in that form, it is now considered one of the most extraordinary pieces in the late 19th-century classical music repertoire. It has been theorized by some musicologists, including Brian Newbould that the symphony's missing fourth movement is actually the *"Entr'acte"* ('Interlude') from Schubert's incidental music to the play, '*Rosamunde*'

To this day, musicologists still debate as to why Schubert left the symphony unfinished. As pointed out earlier, some are of the view that he stopped work in the middle of the scherzo in the fall of 1822 because about this time he came to learn of his initial outbreak of syphilis. There are, however, others who believe that he was perhaps distracted by the inspiration for another creation, the *"Wanderer Fantasy"* for solo

---

[29] Ibid.
[30] Schubert's *"Unfinished Symphony"* is sometimes called the first '*Romantic Symphony*' due to its emphasis on the lyrical impulse within the dramatic structure of Classical sonata form.

piano, which occupied his time and energy immediately afterward. Or, maybe it was a combination of both the factors.

In 1928, the 100th anniversary of Schubert's death, Columbia Records held a worldwide competition for the best conjectural completion of the Unfinished. About 100 completions were submitted, but also a much larger number of original works. The pianist Frank Merrick won the "English Zone" of the competition; his scherzo and finale were later performed and recorded (on Columbia), but are long out of print.[31]

British pianist and Schubert specialist Anthony Goldstone prepared a new 4-movement performing edition of the Symphony for piano duet, using the transcription of the first two movements prepared by Hüttenbrenner, his own completion of Schubert's Scherzo, and the Rosamunde entr'acte in a transcription by Friedrich Hermann, edited by Goldstone. The work in this completed version was given its first recording in 2015 by Goldstone and his wife/duet partner Caroline Clemmow as part of their *'Schubert: Unauthorised Piano Duos'* series for Divine Art Records.

The Russian composer Anton Safronov completed the scherzo sketch and created a new finale for the symphony, which he described as "*an attempt to move into the mind of the composer*". His completion was performed at the Royal Festival Hall in London on 6 November 2007 with the Orchestra of the Age of Enlightenment, [32] and on 2 October 2007 with the Russian National Orchestra, both performances conducted by Vladimir Jurowski. Due to his unusual use of material from Schubert keyboard works in the finale, Safronov's completion has been subject to criticism by music critics.[33]

---

[31] Only some of the completions—Merrick's is not one of them—used material from Schubert's scherzo sketch. The first movement of Joseph Holbrooke's Fourth Symphony, one of the British entries, is mostly a performing version of the sketch, and a theme from the scherzo appears in his finale. Independent completions of the scherzo movement also were made by Geoffrey Bush in 1944 and conductor Denis Vaughan c. 1960. [See, Wikipedia]

[32] Barnett, Laura, "*Arts Diary: Unfinished gets finished*". The Guardian, 11 July 2007.

[33] Shirley, Hugo. "*Stephen Hough; Orchestra of the Age of Enlightenment / Vladimir Jurowski, Weber: Freischütz Overture; Schubert: Symphony No.8 (compl. Safronov); Brahms: Piano Concerto No. 1, Royal Festival Hall, 6 November 2007*". MusicalCriticism.com.

Interestingly, in January 2019, Chinese technology company Huawei used artificial intelligence to create hypothetical melodies for the third and fourth movements, based on which Lucas Cantor arranged an orchestral score. The composition was performed live at Cadogan Hall in London on 4 February 2019. However, many consider that the result is disappointing and far from Schubert's style.[34] Goetz Richter writes, for instance: "*The completed movements are trivial and achieve ultimately a loose and inauthentic family resemblance to Schubert*".[35]

The Unfinished Symphony: In Popular Culture

The "unfinished Symphony" by Franz Schubert has often been used in films and TV shows. The symphony's first movement was used as a leitmotif in the 2002 film directed by Steven Spielberg, *Minority Report*,[36] starring Tom Cruise and Colin Farrell.[37]

Earlier in the 1957 Harvey Films Casper the Friendly Ghost animated short Boo Bop, Casper discovers the ghost of Franz Schubert struggling to "finish" his *"Unfinished Symphony"* at his original piano in a Museum of Music. Schubert's ghost keeps playing the second/celli theme of the first movement on the piano, but is repeatedly distracted, first by Casper and then by outside noises such as a clopping horse, a shooting gallery, construction, and traffic. Casper comes forward to help the ghost of the composer Schubert to complete his "Unfinished Symphony" first, by silencing the offending noises through various

---

[34] Wikipedia

[35] Richter, Goetz. "*Composers are under no threat from AI, if Huawei's finished Schubert symphony is a guide*". The Conversation.

[36] "*Minority Report*" is a 2002 American science fiction action film directed by Steven Spielberg, loosely based on the 1956 novella "*The Minority Report*" by Philip K. Dick. The film is set in Washington, D.C., and Northern Virginia in the year 2054, where Precrime, a specialized police department, apprehends criminals by use of foreknowledge provided by three psychics called "precogs".

[37] Oestreich, James R., "*Schubertizing the Movies*". The New York Times Company. 30 June 2002.

means, and then by inspiring Schubert's ghost to compose past the end of that theme. [38][39]

At the start of the 1979 comic film Being There, directed by Hal Ashby, the character Chance, played by Peter Sellers, wakes as a television remotely snaps on, showing an orchestra performing the *"Unfinished Symphony"*, apparently reflecting on the character's abnormally "unfinished" personality. [40]

In the 1981 TV series Smurfs,[41] the first theme of the first movement has frequently been often used either as the theme song of Gargamel,[42] or in scenes where the Smurfs are in danger.

The Wanderer Fantasy (1822)

> *"[Only] the devil may play it."*
>
> *- Franz Schubert*

The *'Fantasie'* in C major, Op. 15, D. 760, popularly known as the *"Wanderer Fantasy"*, is a four-movement fantasy for solo piano. Widely considered Schubert's most technically demanding composition for the piano, Schubert himself said that only "*the devil may play it,*"-- in reference to his own inability to do so properly.[43]

Schubert composed this work in late 1822, just after breaking off work on the *'Unfinished Symphony'* while sketching its incomplete scherzo.

---

[38] Wikipedia

[39] "Boo Bop". IMDb.

[40] *"Being There"*. IMDb.

[41] The Smurfs is a Belgian comic franchise centered on a fictional colony of small, blue, humanoid creatures who live in mushroom-shaped houses in the forest. The Smurfs was first created and introduced as a series of comic characters by the Belgian comics artist Peyo (the pen name of Pierre Culliford) in 1958. There are more than 100 Smurf characters, and their names are based on adjectives that emphasise their characteristics, such as "Jokey Smurf", who likes to play practical jokes on his fellow Smurfs. The Smurfs wear Phrygian caps, which came to represent freedom during the modern era.

[42] *Gargamel* is a conniving, evil human wizard, driven by a desire for riches and power as well as a bottomless thirst to capture Smurfs. This fixation started long ago when he dreamed of putting a Smurf into his cauldron to make a philosopher's stone, which turns lead into gold.

[43] Duncan, Edmondstoune, *"Schubert"*. J. M. Dent & Co., 1905, p. 165

The piece is in a single movement and is based on a theme from Schubert's own song "*Der Wanderer*" (The Wanderer), which reflects themes of longing, wandering, and introspection.

"*The Wanderer Fantasy*" has had a profound influence on later composers and pianists. Its technical innovations and emotional depth paved the way for the Romantic piano music that followed, including the works of Franz Liszt and Johannes Brahms.

Liszt was so fascinated by the '*Wanderer Fantasy*' that he transcribed it for piano and orchestra (S.366) and two pianos (S.653). He also edited the original score and added some various interpretations in ossia [44], and made a complete rearrangement of the final movement.

Franz Liszt

---

[44] '*Ossia*' is a musical term for an alternative passage that may be played instead of the original passage. Ossia passages are very common in opera and solo-piano works. They are usually an easier version of the preferred form of passage.

The piano solo music of Franz Liszt is typically full of 'ossia', often no easier or more difficult than the rest of the piece. This reflects Liszt's desire to leave his options open during a performance.

Many celebrated pianists have taken on the challenge of performing "*The Wanderer Fantasy*." Notable interpretations have been given by artists such as Alfred Brendel, Sviatoslav Richter, and Maurizio Pollini.

The piece's exploration of themes like wandering and longing has resonated with audiences for generations. It captures the Romantic era's fascination with the individual's inner emotional world and the idea of the wandering, searching soul. The "Wanderer" theme that serves as the basis for the piece's variations can be seen as a representation of the artist's existential journey, a recurring theme in Romantic literature and music.

By late 1822, Schubert was in severe mental distress. With his financial needs remaining unfulfilled, and publishers and opera house owners still reluctant to accept his works, he was at his wits' end and did not really know what to do.

About this time, Schubert entered yet another dark phase of his life as he became critically ill; historians believe that about this time he almost certainly contracted syphilis. For him, the following year 1823, was, one of illness and retirement. And yet, Schubert continued to produce at a prolific rate. In April, he made another attempt to gain success in Viennese theatres with the one-act operetta *"Die Verschworenen"* ('The Conspirators'), D. 787; the title was changed later because of political censorship - to *"Der häusliche Krieg"* ('Domestic Warfare'). During the year, Schubert also composed, amongst other works, the drama "*Rosamunde'*, the opera " *Fierrabras*", and one of his greatest masterpieces -- the famous cycle of songs called "*Die Schone Mullerin*"('The Beautiful Maid of the Mill'), representing the epitome of Schubert's lyrical art.. Many of the songs belonging to it were written while he was in the hospital for treatment of syphilis.

Die schöne Müllerin ('The Beautiful Maid of the Mill') *(1823)*

Considered one of Schubert's most important works, "*Die schöne Müllerin*", Op. 25, D. 795, ('The Beautiful Maid of the Mill'), a song cycle, composed in 1823, based on poems by the German poet Wilhelm Muller (1794-1827) is the first of his two seminal cycles (the other being his later '*Winterreise*'), and a pinnacle of lied.[45] It is performed by a pianist and a solo singer. The piano bears much of the expressive burden of the work and is not a mere 'accompaniment' to the singer. The cycle is known for its emotional depth, beautiful melodies, and its ability to capture the essence of Romanticism.

Wilhelm Muller

Müller's poems were published in 1820, and Schubert set most of them to music between May and September 1823, while he was also writing his opera '*Fierrabras*'. He was 26 years old at the time. Schubert omitted five of the poems. It is widely performed and recorded. The work was published in 1824 by Sauer and Leidesdorf as Op. 25.

---

[45] The collection of poems "*The Beautiful Müller*" by Wilhelm Müller, is included in the *Seven and Seventy Posthumous Poems from the Papers of a Traveling French Horn Playe*r, published in 1821. Schubert set 20 of the 25 poems to music, which eliminated the poet's intended irony in the romantic sense and the pessimistic conclusion. The content refers - according to biographical sources and letters - to Müller's unfulfilled love for Luise Hensel. [See, Ernst Hilmar: *Franz Schubert*. Rowohlt, Hamburg 1997, p. 97; Also, see Wikipedia: "*The beautiful Miller*"]

There are twenty songs in the cycle, and they move from cheerful optimism to despair and tragedy. At the beginning of the cycle, a young worker who wanders happily through the countryside comes upon a brook, which he follows to a mill. He falls in love with the miller's beautiful daughter. She is out of his reach as he is only a worker. He tries to impress her, but her response seems tentative. The young man is soon supplanted in her affections by a hunter clad in green -- the colour of a ribbon he gave the girl. In his anguish, he experiences an obsession with the colour green, and then an extravagant death fantasy in which flowers sprout from his grave to express his undying love (as in Beethoven's *"Adelaide"* for a similar fantasy). In the end, the young man in despair drowns himself in the brook. The last number is a lullaby sung by the brook.

"*Die schöne Müllerin*" has been widely performed and recorded by various vocalists and pianists over the years. It's considered one of Schubert's masterpieces and an essential work in the art song (Lied) repertoire. The cycle has received critical acclaim for its emotional depth and Schubert's ability to capture the nuances of the text through music. The earliest evidence of a performance of several songs in the cycle is a program note in the University Library of Breslau: On December 16, 1825, the baritone Johann Theodor Mosewius performed the contents of the first volume (Nos. 1–4) as part of a musical evening entertainment in the Breslau large Provincial resource. [46] Most probably, Carl von Schönstein and Johann Michael Vogl also performed parts of the Müller in a smaller or larger setting during Schubert's lifetime. The first cyclical performance by Julius Stockhausen in Vienna is recorded in 1856, who also performed it in 1861 (in Hamburg with Brahms on the piano) and in 1866 with Anton Rubinstein in Russia. This long period of over 30 years was, to an extent, due to the performance practice common in the 19th century,

---

[46] Till Gerrit Waidelich: "*Unknown Schubert documents from Breslau*". In: Schubert: Perspectives, 8, 2008, Stuttgart 2009, pp. 17 48,

which often preferred a varied program of individual movements or songs to the performance of entire works and cycles. [47]

The cycle has had a lasting impact on the world of classical music. It set a precedent for future song cycles and expanded the possibilities for vocal and piano composition. Its influence can be seen in the works of later composers, such as Robert Schumann and Johannes Brahms, who also composed significant Lieder.

In addition to its performance in its original form, "*Die schöne Müllerin*" has been adapted and reinterpreted in various ways, including through dance, theater, and visual art. Some notable interpreters include Dietrich Fischer-Dieskau, Fritz Wunderlich, and Ian Bostridge, among others. This highlights its enduring appeal and the universality of its themes.

Six of the songs of "*Die schöne Müllerin*" were transcribed for solo piano by Franz Liszt and published as '*Mueller lieder'*.

In literature, "*Die schöne Müllerin*" has often served as a motif, for example in the novel "*The Butterfly Catcher*" by Sabine M. Gruber , which uses the song cycle as a framework in terms of content and form.

In 2001, Christoph Marthaler directed *Die schöne Müllerin*" at the *Schauspielhaus* Zurich; the production was later invited to the Berlin *Theatertreffen*. Also in 2001, Bärenreiter-Verlag published a choral version (SATB) of the work, which was prepared by Carlo Marenco.

Fierrabras (1823)

In 1823, Schubert composed "*Fierrabras*", D 796, a three-act German opera, with its music set to a text by the Austrian poet and Secretary at the Kärntnertortheater, Josef Kupelweiser. Along with the earlier "*Alfonso und Estrella*" composed in 1822, it marks Schubert's yet another attempt to compose grand Romantic opera in German, departing from the singspiel (sing-play) tradition.

---

[47] Susan Youens: "*Schubert – The Beautiful Miller*". Cambridge University Press, 1992, p. 22.

The libretto by Kupelwieser is about the adventures of the is about the adventures of the Moorish Knight Fierrabras, and his eventual conversion to Christianity. It is based on a folk-lore as to how Fierrabras's sister falls in love with a Knight of King Charlemagne (Charles the Great) -- and the love between Charlemagne's daughter Emma and another of his knights, Eginhard. Kupelwieser had likely drawn his inspiration from German publications of the tales of Charlemagne, including an 1806 translation *"La puente de Mantible"* ('The Bridge of Mantible') by Calderón.

In 1822 the Kärntnertortheater commissioned operas from Schubert and Carl Maria von Weber, the famous German composer, in a bid to increase the number of German operas in repertoire. This became necessary for the Kärntnertor Theater was facing a problem at that time. The contract for the opera that was running in the theater at that time was about to be over and, given the prevailing mood of the public authorities against Italian influence in opera, it was certainly not to be renewed. Only a year ago, in 1821, the Italian impresario, Domenico Barbaja[48], an ambitious former coffeehouse waiter who by gambling and running a gaming house had amassed a fortune, had taken over the *Kärntnertortheater* -- he was, therefore, in search of a new opera that would ensure the house some prosperity. Schubert's friend and an ardent admirer Josef Hüttenbrenner and others had acclaimed Schubert

---

[48] Born on 10 August 1777 in Milan, Barbaja began his career by running a coffee shop. He made his first fortune by creating a special kind of coffee with frothing milk, the *"Barbajada"*, probably the first "cappuccino." This drink, and a variation with hot chocolate like *"Bicerin"*, became so popular in Milan that the erstwhile waiter was able to open a string of coffee houses in the city that all featured his novel concoction.

Barbaia made his second fortune by buying and selling munitions during the Napoleonic wars. After the French re-allowed gambling as they advanced southwards in Italy, he became involved in the operations as a card dealer at the "La Scala" opera house but soon gained the position to run the entire gaming operation of the house and gradually extended his network Naples.

By 1809, he took over the "Teatro di San Carlo", the major opera house, as well as the second royal theatre, the "Nuovo", and two additional ones in Naples. From 1821, he became also the manager of two theatres in Vienna, the *"Kärntnertortheater"* and the *"Theater an der Wien"*. In 1826 he took over the running of *"La Scala"*, before returning to Naples.

to him, but all their good words about him fell only on deaf ears. Barbaja had no faith in Schubert. *"This man is a songwriter"*, he declared. *"What does he know of opera?"* But he commissioned Schubert to write an opera for his house nonetheless.

Domenico Barbaja

Schubert was ecstatic. Swift to the new chance, he completed the whole of the work, approximately one thousand pages of music, in four months, between May 23 and September 25, 1823. The opera when complete was delivered to Barbaja, who, owing to his preoccupation with other work, put it in a drawer and forgot it. Schubert's repeated requests for a verdict on his four month's work were ignored.

Apparently, fate had something else in store for the young composer. Weber, on the one hand, was ready to stage his opera *"Euryanthe"*, while Schubert, on his part, was prepared with *"Fierrabras"*. But something strange happened.

At that time, Rossini, the celebrated Italian composer, particularly known for both comic and serious opera, was very popular throughout Europe. After Barbaja had taken over the *Kärntnertortheater* the year before, he invited the sensational Rossini to Vienna to stage his operas at his Theater. Rossini's operas had been so popular in Vienna that when, after he his departure, Weber's *"Euryanthe"* was premiered in October 1823, it was commercially not a success. And it spelt disaster for Schubert -- Barbaja quietly shelved the plan to stage *"Fierrabras"*.

Gioachino Antonio Rossini

Barbaja returned Schubert's work stating that its production was impossible because of the poor quality of the libretto. Thus the enthusiasm for an opera which Schubert had regarded as certain of public performance suddenly went for a toss; he was left only with a bundle of manuscript and no chance of production.

This was an unexpected blow to Schubert. An aggrieved Kupelwieser resigned from the post of Secretary at the Kärntnertortheater, complaining of "arrogance" on the part of Barbaja. Most unfortunately for Schubert, he never saw his opera staged, nor did he receive any payment for the work.

Leopold Kupelwieser

An embittered Schubert, in a letter dated March 31, 1824, wrote to the Austrian painter and his friend Leopold Kupelwieser (younger brother of Josef Kupelweiser) who was in Rome:

> "...*every night when I go to sleep, I hope that I may never wake up again. Yet every day, the morning breaks into the pains of yesterday's wounds...*"

> "... *I feel myself the most unhappy, most wretched being in the world. Figure to yourself a man whose health will never come right again, and who in his despair at this is always making things worse instead of better; a man whose most brilliant hopes have come to nothing, to whom the happiness of love and friendship offers nothing but sorrow, whom the feeling (the inspiring feeling at least) for the beautiful threatens to abandon; and ask yourself if he is not wretched, unhappy? My peace is gone, my heart is heavy; I shall find it never, and never more; I can say daily, for every night when I go to sleep, I hope that I may never wake up again. Yet every day, the morning breaks into the pains of yesterday's wounds.*"

On May 7, 1835, seven years after Schubert's death, a concert version of several numbers of *'Fierrabras'* was staged at the *'Theater in der Josefstadt'*[49] in Vienna. Schubert's music was highly acclaimed, but the work was generally considered to suffer from an extremely weak libretto.

Many years later, in 1897, its first full performance was given at the *'Hoftheater Karlsruhe'*('The Grand Ducal Court Theater in Karlsruhe')under the direction of the Austrian conductor and composer Felix Mottl, edited for the taste of the day.[50][51]

Felix Mottl

---

[49] The *"Theater in der Josefstadt"* is a theatre in Vienna in the eighth district of Josefstadt. It was founded in 1788 and is the oldest still performing theater in Vienna.

[50] Flower, Newman: *"Franz Schubert - The Man and His Circle"*, Tudor Publishing Co., New York, December, 1935.

[51] *"Letter to Leopold Kupelwieser"*, March 31, 1824: Reprinted in *"Music in the Romantic Era"* by Alfred Einstein, W.W. Norton & Company, (1 April, 1947).

A scene from *'Fierrabras'*

Rosamunde (1823)

The same year, in 1823, Schubert also composed the incidental music of "*Rosamunde, Fürstin von Zypern*" ('Rosamunde, Princess of Cyprus'), D. 644 -- a play by German journalist, poet and playwright Helmina von Chezy. It was premiered in Vienna's '*Theater an der Wien*' on 20 December 1823. The play itself was not successful, but Schubert's music has become famous in its own right.

Helmina von Chezy

The play is about the attempt of Rosamunde, Princess of Cyprus', who was brought up incognito as a shepherdess by the mariner's widow Axa, to reclaim her throne from the Governor Fulgentius, who had poisoned her parents. Rosamunde's claim is backed by a deed in her father's hand; she also enjoys the support of Cypriots and the Cretan Prince Alfonso, her betrothed. Finally, all the attempts of Fulgentius to kill her fail; he dies by his own poison, and Rosamunde ascends the throne.

'*Rosamunde*' was performed only twice in 1823, but then the original manuscript was lost. It was rediscovered by George Grove, the leading English musicologist and Editor of Grove's "*Dictionary of Music and Musicians*" and the English composer Sir Arthur Sullivan when they visited Vienna in 1867, specifically to research on Schubert. Grove wrote:

George Grove   Sir Arthur Sullivan

"*I found, at the bottom of the cupboard, and in its farthest corner, a bundle of music-books two feet high, carefully tied round, and black with the undisturbed dust of nearly half-a-century. ... These were the part-books of the whole of the music in Rosamunde, tied up after the second performance in*

December, 1823, and probably never disturbed since. Dr. Schneider [Schubert's nephew] *must have been amused at our excitement; ... at any rate, he kindly overlooked it, and gave us permission to take away with us and copy what we wanted."*

Grove says they were nearly smothered with dust in digging it out of the musical catacombs; but when they found the manuscript, they were so overjoyed that they copied scores until two in the morning. Then, in the night air, they played a game of leapfrog around the room.

Schubert's incidental music in *'Rosamunde'* is scored for orchestra – and for some of the numbers-- for diverse combinations of singers. Excerpts from the Rosamunde music are frequently performed and are amongst Schubert's most performed pieces. The most well-known piece from this music is the "*Rosamunde Overture*" (Overture No. 3 in D major, D. 644), which is often performed as a standalone concert piece. It's a lively and engaging composition that showcases Schubert's melodic prowess.[52]

The overture was used for a ballet sequence in the 1952 Samuel Goldwyn film *'Hans Christian Anderson'*, starring Danny Kaye. Another excerpt was incorporated into a popular Christmas Carol. It has also been played in Marvel's film *'The Avengers'* in the German opera house scene.

So, none of Schubert's finished pieces -- each one a rare musical masterpiece in its own right -- brought him the fortune he deserved or so greatly needed. A hapless Schubert, battling health problems, again turned to music for escape.

But he was in desperate need of money, particularly because he had to pay the bills for his medical care that was quite expensive. So in May 1824, he returned to his private teaching job with the Esterházy family

---

[52] Music educators often use classic compositions like the "*Rosamunde Overture*" as teaching material for students, which can influence the next generation of musicians and composers. Musicians who arrange or orchestrate classical works for different ensembles or settings are also often inspired by Schubert's compositions, including the "*Rosamunde Overture*," and incorporate elements of his style into their arrangements.

and went again to Zseliz. The quiet beauty and enjoyment of this country retreat, the kindness and appreciation shown to him by the family worked well on his spirits; and during his stay there, he produced several important compositions. In 1824 he turned out, amongst other compositions, three chamber works, the "*String Quartet in A minor,*" a second "*String quartet in D minor*" and "*Octet in F Major*" for strings and wind instruments.

String Quartet No. 13 in A minor (**'Rosamunde' Quartet**) *(1824)*

Starting in 1824, Schubert largely turned away from the composition of songs to concentrate on instrumental chamber music. As a part of this endeavour, he returned to the string quartet form that he had last visited when he wrote the one-movement "*Quartettsatz"* in 1820.

Between February and March 1824, Schubert wrote the String Quartet No. 13 in A minor, D 804, Op. 29, also known as "*Rosamunde*" quartet". It was written using a theme from the incidental music he wrote for the play "Rosamunde" that failed.[53] The quartet consists of four movements which last around 30 minutes in total.

Schubert dedicated the work to Ignaz Schuppanzigh, one of the leading violinists of the time and who had served as the first violinist of the string quartet composed by Beethoven. Schuppanzigh himself played in the premiere performance of Schubert's "Rosamunde" quartet, which took place on 14 March 1824.

Schubert's chamber music, including the "Rosamunde Quartet," played a crucial role in the development of Romantic-era chamber music. His works in this genre have had a lasting impact on subsequent composers. The quartet's themes have been featured in various films, television shows, and other media, contributing to its cultural recognition.

---

[53] The nickname "Rosamunde" was not given by Schubert himself, and it's associated with this quartet due to its use in the play.

The "Rosamunde Quartet" is considered one of Schubert's most popular and frequently performed string quartets. It is characterized by its lyrical melodies and expressive, often melancholic, themes, which are typical of Schubert's style. The quartet is admired for its emotional depth and the beauty of its melodies, making it a beloved work among chamber music enthusiasts.

String Quartet No. 14 in D minor ['Death and the Maiden'] *(1824)*

Within weeks of completing *"Rosamunde"* quartet, in March 1824 Schubert composed another masterpiece -- the D minor quartet, D. 810 -- *"Death and the Maiden"*.[54] Alongside the 'Rosamunde' Quartet, Death and the Maiden marks a radical break with Schubert's previous works in this genre. Whereas his earlier quartets more or less followed in the footsteps of Haydn and Mozart, *"Death and the Maiden"* reflects a determination to stamp his own individuality on the medium. It was first played in January 1826 at the Vienna home of Karl and Franz Hacker, amateur violinists, with Schubert on the viola. It was published by Diabelli in 1831, three years after Schubert's death.

Considered "*one of the pillars of the chamber music repertoire*", the quartet takes its name from the lied *"Der Tod und das Madchen"*, a setting of the poem of the same name by German poet Matthias Claudius that Schubert wrote in 1817. The theme of the song forms the basis of the second movement of the quartet. The theme is a death knell that accompanies the song about the terror and comfort of death. It is sometimes reckoned as Schubert's *"testament to death"*.

> The Maiden:
>
> "*Oh! leave me! Prithee, leave me! thou grisly man of bone!*
>
> *For life is sweet, is pleasant.*

---

[54] The nickname "*Death and the Maiden*" was not given by Schubert but was later attached to the quartet due to its second movement, which is based on his earlier lied "*Death and the Maiden*" (D. 531, Op. 7, No. 3).

> *Go! leave me now alone!*
>
> *Go! leave me now alone!"*

Death:

> *"Give me thy hand, oh! maiden fair to see,*
>
> *For I'm a friend, hath ne'er distress'd thee.*
>
> *Take courage now, and very soon*
>
> *Within mine arms shalt softly rest thee!"*[55]

Schubert composed the quartet in 1824, after he had become seriously ill and realized that his days were numbered. The quartet is often associated with Schubert's awareness of his own mortality.

These quartets, like, *"Rosamunde"* or *"Death and the Maiden"* are qualitatively far superior to Schubert's initial attempts, like, *"Quartettsatz"* in 1820. Even Schubert recognized this fact; in July 1824 he wrote to his brother Ferdinand of his earlier quartets, "*it would be better if you stuck to other quartets than mine, for there is nothing in them...*"

There are several qualities that set apart these mature quartets from his earlier attempts. These are structurally much more integrated, with motifs, harmonies, and textures recurring in a way that ties the entire work together

---

[55] Translation by P. Jurgenson, c. 1920 in Chaliapin c. 1920, p. 40. The translation is somewhat free, here is a more literal rendering:

The Maiden:

"*Away! Ah, Away! thou cruel man of bone!*

I am still young. Go, instead.

And do not touch me!"

Death:

"*Give me thy hand, you fair and tender creature,*

I'm a friend, and do not come to punish.

Be of good courage; I am not cruel

You shall sleep gently in my arms."

After the initial rendering of the *"Death and the Maiden"* quartet in 1826, it was played again at a house concert in the home of Schubert's friend and composer Franz Lachner. Ignatius Schuppanzigh, the famous violinist, friend and teacher of Beethoven, who debuted many of Beethoven's and Schubert's quartets, was leading the composition; and he was reportedly unimpressed. *"Brother, this is nothing at all, let well alone: stick to your Lieder,"* the aging Schuppanzigh is believed to have said to Schubert.

Ignatius Schuppanzigh

But contrary to Schuppanzigh's opinion, *"Death and the Maiden"* soon occupied a leading place on the concert stage and won the hearts of music lovers and other connoisseurs of music. Today, it is considered one of the pillars of the chamber music repertoire. In the words of Robert Schumann, the great German composer:

> *"Only the excellence of such a work as Schubert's D minor Quartet... can in any way console us for the early and grievous death of this first-born of Beethoven; in a few years he achieved and perfected things as no one before him"*

Schubert's late quartets, including the *"Death and the Maiden,"* were groundbreaking in their harmonic and structural innovations. They had a significant influence on later composers like Gustav Mahler, Antonín Dvořák, and Dmitri Shostakovich.

The quartet consists of four movements[56]:

    I. Allegro[57]

    II. Andante con moto[58] (based on the "Death and the Maiden" theme)

    III. Scherzo: Allegro molto[59]

    IV. Presto[60]

Death and the Maiden" is considered one of Schubert's masterpieces and is highly regarded for its emotional depth and innovative use of thematic material. The second movement is particularly famous for its variations on the song's melody. The quartet's haunting and melancholic character has made it a favorite among both musicians and audiences.

---

[56] The quartet begins with a unison D, played fortissimo, and a triplet figure, that establishes the triplet motif. After the introduction, Schubert presents the first theme: a continuation of the chorale motif, but with the triplet motif rippling through the lower voices, in a restless, unremitting stream.

The second movement is a theme and five variations, based on the theme from the Schubert Lied. The theme is like a death march in G minor, ending on a G major chord. Throughout the movement, Schubert does not deviate from the basic harmonic and sentence structure of the 24-measure theme. But each variation expresses a profoundly different emotion.

Cobbett describes the third movement as the "*dance of the demon fiddler*".[See Cobbett, Walter Willson, ed. (1929). Cobbett's Cyclopedic Survey of Chamber Music. Oxford University Press., v.2, p.359] There is indeed something demonic in this fast-paced scherzo, full of syncopations and, like the other movements, dramatic leaps from fortissimo to pianissimo.

The finale of the quartet is a tarantella in rondo-sonata form, in D minor. [See, Wikipedia]

[57] Allegro (Italian: 'lively'): Meaning the music should be played cheerfully. Upbeat and brisk.

[58] Andante con moto: Slowly, but with motion. This direction informs the performer that whilst the music should be slow, it should not be so slow that things grind to a halt. There should be some sense of motion in the music.

[59] Allegro molto is an Italian term used to describe when music is played in a very swift and lively fashion, or tempo. The speed is between 132-152 beats per minute.

[60] In music, to play something presto is to play it at a very fast tempo. Presto comes from Italian for "quickly." Officially, presto is the second-quickest speed that music can be played (after prestissimo).

"*Death and the Maiden*" is frequently performed in concert and has been recorded by many renowned string quartets. Some famous interpretations include those by the Amadeus Quartet, the Alban Berg Quartet, and the Emerson String Quartet.

The quartet has also inspired works such as, Chilean playwright Ariel Dorfman's 1991 play '*Death and the Maiden*', adapted for film in 1994 by Roman Polanski. In this play, Paulina Salas, a former political prisoner in a Latin American country, is raped by her captors, led by a sadistic doctor whose face she never saw. The rapist doctor plays Schubert's String Quartet No. 14during the act of rape;

The quartet has also appeared as incidental music in numerous films: '*The Portrait of a Lady*' (Jane Campion, 1996), '*What?*'(Roman Polanski, 1972), '*Sherlock Holmes and the Case of the Silk Stocking*' (BBC production, 2004), and in Samuel Beckett's radio play '*All That Fall*' (1962).

At the state funeral of the Norwegian explorer, Fridtj of Nansen, in 1930, '*Death and the Maiden*' was performed instead of speeches.

Octet in F major (1824)

The same month, in March 1824, he composed "Death and the Maiden", Schubert also completed his *"Octet in F major, D 803"*. It was a remarkable feat considering that he was quite unwell at that time and was under medical treatment.

Schubert composed the Octet on being commissioned by Austrian noble, philanthropist, and renowned clarinetist Cardinal Ferdinand Julius von Troyer to write a companion piece of Beethoven's popular E-flat Septet. In his composition, Schubert enriched the seven-part instrumentation of Beethoven's septet with an additional violin to create an Octet.

Cardinal Ferdinand Julius von Troyer

The Octet was created in only a few weeks of February and March 1824 and was first performed in April 1824 at the residence of Troyer's employer, the Archduke Rudolf of Austria -- to whom Beethoven's '*Archduke Trio*' is dedicated. Troyer himself played the clarinet part at the premier and it included many of the musicians who participated in the first performance of the Septet.

Although Schubert's operas remained unperformed, his songs had by this time become quite popular in Vienna; so he would have frequent public performances during these and the following years. His financial position, therefore, though still strained, had somewhat improved.

In the summer of 1825, Schubert began to compose his famous '*Ninth Symphony*', which was completed by the next summer. He was on a creative spree. In course of the year, he composed piano sonatas in A Minor and in D Major, numerous songs including the popular "*Lady of the Lake*" and the famous "*Ave Maria*".

Chapter 7
The Musical journey – Later years
(1825-1827)

Ave Maria (1825)

In 1825 Schubert composed "*Ellens dritter Gesang*", ("Ellen's Third Song"), D. 839, a setting of seven songs from Sir Walter Scott's popular epic poem *"The Lady of the Lake"*- a long wandering poem set in the highlands with caves, warriors, harps and rebellions. These were published in 1826 as his Opus 52.

Sir Walter Scott

The opening words and refrain of Ellen's song, namely "*Ave Maria*" (Latin for "Hail Mary"), most possibly led to adapting Schubert's melody as a setting for the traditional Roman Catholic prayer "*Ave Maria*" (which is a prayer to Virgin Mary). Schubert, however, did not originally write the musical piece with religious practices or the Catholic church in mind though there are some misconceptions that he wrote the melody as a setting for the Latin "*Ave Maria*".

Considered one of the most beautiful and inspired melodies ever written, it is one of Schubert's most popular works and has been recorded by a wide range of artists, from Perry Como to Pavarotti to Andrea Bocelli,[61] under the title of "*Ave Maria*". It was arranged in three versions for piano by the Hungarian virtuoso, Franz Liszt.

Andrea Bocelli – singing the beautiful "*Ave Maria*" in St. Stephens Basilica in Budapest

'*Ave Maria*' was first performed at the castle of Countess Sophie Weissenwolff in the little town of Styregg in Upper Austria. Schubert dedicated it to the Countess that led to her popularly known as "*the Lady of the Lake*".

Even during Schubert's brief lifetime, "*Ave Maria*" was considered a masterpiece, and, unlike the vast majority of his compositions, it found a publisher before his death.

"*Ave Maria*" is frequently performed at weddings, religious ceremonies, and other special occasions. It has been arranged for various voice types, including soprano, tenor, and instrumental ensembles, which allows for a wide range of interpretations. Various

---

[61] "*...if God would have a singing voice, he must sound a lot like Andrea Bocelli*" -- Canadian singer Celine Dion.

musicians and composers have created adaptations of Schubert's original composition, which has contributed to its enduring popularity.

The great American entrepreneur, animator and film producer Walt Disney used Schubert's song in the final part of his 1940 film *'Fantasia'*.

Walt Disney

American-born violinist and conductor Yehudi Menuhin, widely considered one of the greatest violinists of the 20th century, performed a version of *'Ave Maria'* for violin and piano in the 1943 American musical film *'Stage Door Canteen'*.

Yehudi Menuhin

The song has been used in several films including, '*Bride of Frankenstein*' (1935), the Academy Award-winning film '*Going My Way*' (1944) and the science fiction film '*2BR02B: To Be or Naught to Be*' (2016) -- just to name a few.

"*Ave Maria*" holds deep spiritual and cultural significance, and it is often performed in religious settings. The piece's gentle and reverent character evokes feelings of devotion and serenity, making it a poignant choice for moments of reflection and prayer.

Schubert's "*Ave Maria*" is a timeless and universally adored composition. Its profound spirituality and captivating melody have made it a staple in both classical music and religious contexts, and it continues to be treasured by audiences around the world.

The song was performed by Boston tenor Luigi Vena at the funeral of American president John F. Kennedy.

1826: Schubert fails again to get a job

In 1824, Salieri had resigned as Imperial Kapellmeister following which his deputy, Josef Eybler, was promoted to that post. In 1826, Schubert applied for the vacant post of Vice-Kapellmeister at the Stadtkonvikt with the following application addressed to the Emperor Francis II:

> *"Your Majesty!*
>
> *Most gracious Emperor!*
>
> *With the deepest submission the undersigned humbly begs Your Majesty graciously to bestow upon him the vacant position of Vice-Kapellmeister to the Court, and supports his application with the following qualifications:*
>
>> *(1) The undersigned was born in Vienna, is the son of a school teacher, and is of 29 years of age.*
>>
>> *(2) He enjoyed the privilege of being for five years a Court Chorister at the Imperial and Royal College School.*

(3) He received a complete course of instruction in composition from the late Chief Kapellmeister to the Court, Herr Anton Salieri, and is fully qualified, therefore, to fill any post as Kapellmeister.

(4) His name is well known, not only in Vienna but throughout Germany, as a composer of songs and instrumental music.

(5) He has also written and arranged five Masses for both smaller and larger orchestras, and these have already been performed in various churches in Vienna.

(6) Finally, he is at the present time without employment, and hopes in the security of a permanent position to be able to realize at last those high musical aspirations which he has ever kept before him.

Should Your Majesty be graciously pleased to grant this request, the undersigned would strive to the utmost to give full satisfaction.

Your Majesty's most obedient humble servant,

Franz Schubert"

Though he was undoubtedly the top candidate, he did not get the job. The young genius had no friend or well-wisher near the seat of powers that be, and after a year the job was given to someone else. Schubert had only two more years to live. [62]

From then until his death, Schubert seems to have let matters drift. It appears as if he had become aware of his humble birth and upbringing. This made him diffident, and hesitant. He was disappointed and sad -- though it was no new experience for him. But his indomitable creative

---

[62] Schuster, Lincoln M.: *"The World's Great Letters"*, Simon and Schuster Inc., Rockefeller Center, New York City, New York, 1940, p. 266-267.

spirit kept him alive. The rest of his life he almost entirely devoted to composition.

Schubert was a victim of misfortune, lack of recognition and unwarranted rejections throughout his life; It is, therefore, no wonder he once wrote: *"Man resembles a ball, to be played with by fate and chance."*

By this time, his health was also failing; he was to live for barely two more years. While listening to his last few compositions, one experiences the feeling that he perhaps had the premonition of death approaching him -- much stronger than in Mozart's music. His last Mass is an expression of a transcendental vision -- a moving example of how far he had distanced himself from all matters on earth waiting calmly for eternal peace.

The musical journey continues (1826)

Schubert failed to get the job; nevertheless his fortune during this period began to improve. His impressive musical output now continued at an amazing pace, and his popularity in Vienna increased. He was also in negotiations with four different publishers.

1826 was yet another year of several significant works of Schubert. The songs he composed during the year include the settings of Shakespeare's *"Hark! Hark! the lark"* and *"Who is Sylvia?"* written during a brief stay in the village of Währing.

Despite his failing health, in June 1826 Schubert composed, just within a span of ten days, his last string quartet --- the vast and mellifluous "*String Quartet No. 15 in G major*". The same year he also composed the melodically blooming G major piano sonata, sometimes called the "*Fantasie*".

String Quartet No. 15 in G major (1826)

In June 1826, Schubert also composed his famous "*String Quartet No. 15*" in G major, D 887", which is regarded as one of his most profound chamber works. But it could not be published during his life time. It had its premiere in Vienna in 1850, more than two decades after Schubert's death, and thereafter it was posthumously published in 1851 as Opus 161.

The quartet is written for the standard string quartet ensemble, consisting of two violins, a viola, and a cello. The quartet is divided into four movements, following the traditional structure of a classical string quartet. It is known for its length and emotional depth. It is one of the longest string quartets in the standard repertoire, and it typically takes over 40 minutes to perform.

Schubert's String Quartet No. 15 is highly regarded for its emotional intensity and its departure from the typical classical quartet style. It is sometimes considered a bridge between the Classical and Romantic eras of music. The quartet is characterized by its harmonic richness and thematic development. Schubert's use of modulations and harmonic progressions in this work is particularly striking.

In Woody Allen's 1989 comedy-drama *"Crime and Misdemeanors"*, parts of the music from Schubert's '*String Quartet No. 15*'are used to create almost terrifying dramatic effect during several scenes of the crime plot. This was Schubert's last quartet, and it was as if his declamation of love lost, the inevitability of death, and the horror of loneliness.

In *"Gramophone"*, a London based magazine on classical music, Stephen Johnson, the British music journalist and broadcaster for BBC Radio 3, 4 and World Service, referred to the work as Schubert's greatest string quartet, and was of the view that it is heard less frequently than the composer's previous two quartets not because of lower quality but because it is less accessible.

Schubert's String Quartet No. 15 is considered a masterwork of the chamber music repertoire. Its depth and emotional intensity make it a rewarding but challenging piece for both performers and audiences. It stands as a testament to Schubert's creative genius and his ability to blend classical form with Romantic expression. It is a work of great beauty and profundity and remains an important part of the string quartet repertoire.

The Piano Sonata in G major ('Fantasie') *(1826)*

The same year, in October 1826, Schubert completed the *"Piano Sonata in G major"* D. 894, Op. 78 -- a sonata for solo piano-- sometimes called the "Fantasie". It was the last of Schubert's sonatas published during his lifetime.

It is a cruel fact that much of the output of Franz Schubert languished unpublished for years after his death at the age of 31. Of Schubert's 12 complete solo piano sonatas (and almost as many incomplete sonata fragments), only three saw publication during the composer's lifetime, the *Sonata in G major*, D. 894 being the last. Eclipsed by Beethoven's work in the medium, Schubert's sonatas fell into obscurity for nearly a century before being recovered by pianists and audiences.

Schubert's Sonata in G major, D. 894 was first published in 1827 as *Fantasie, Andante, Menuetto und Allegretto*, Op. 78. The title "*Fantasie*" was given by the publisher Tobias Haslinger to the first movement of the work. It was a publisher's decision, perhaps to make the music more commercially appealing as a collection of individual pieces rather than one large composition. Decades later it would still be referred to as the "*Fantasia*" Sonata.

The nickname "*Fantasie*" or "*Fantasy*" sonata stems from its unconventional structure and the sense of improvisation that is interwoven throughout the piece. The work does not adhere strictly to the traditional sonata-allegro form, which was more typical for classical piano sonatas.

Schubert's *Piano Sonata in G major* is celebrated for its unique and innovative structure. The work seems to flow seamlessly from one movement to the next, with interconnected themes and transitions that defy traditional boundaries. This gives it a "fantasy" or improvisatory quality, hence its nickname. The sonata is marked by its emotional depth, shifting moods, and the characteristic Schubertian lyricism. The sonata is of moderate length, typically taking around 20-25 minutes to perform.

The English pianist and Schubert scholar Imogen Cooper has described the G major sonata as "*one of the rare completely serene sonatas*" composed by Schubert, adding, "*Of course, as ever with him, there are contrasting passages which become stormy and a little bit dark, but the overall mood is one of peace and luminosity, in a way that the G Major string quartet, written a few months before, was most definitely not*". She noted further that "*the last movement has tremendous wit in it — and one or two moments of great poignancy, as if a cloud suddenly covered the sun, and then the sun comes out again*".[63]

Imogen Cooper

Schubert's *Piano Sonata in G major*, D. 894, is a captivating composition that showcases his ability to blend classical structures with Romantic expressiveness and innovation. Its nickname "*Fantasie*" aptly describes the piece's free-form character, and it remains a beloved part of the piano repertoire for both performers and listeners.

---

[63] "*Imogen Cooper interview on BBC Radio 3*", included in broadcast of Schubert piano recital on May 1, 2009

Robert Schumann, the great German composer of the Romantic era, described it as the "*most perfect in form and conception*" of any of Schubert's sonatas.[64]

1827: Death of Ludwig van Beethoven

> "...who can hope to do anything after Beethoven"
>
> - Franz Schubert

The year 1827 began on a grim note that nearly shook the music world. Ludwig van Beethoven, heralded as one of the greatest and most influential composers of all time – the predominant musical figure in the transitional period between the Classical and Romantic eras -- was on death bed.

Ludwig van Beethoven

Beethoven suffered declining health throughout the last years of his life. In late 1826, illness struck again, with prolonged episodes of vomiting and diarrhea that nearly ended his life.

During early December of 1826, after a two-day trip in an open cart, Beethoven developed pneumonia. Thereafter, he rarely left his bed. He was afflicted, among other things, with fluid collecting in his body. To relieve the abdominal swelling, the doctors performed four minor

---

[61] "*Piano Sonata in G major, D 894 (Schubert)*", Wikipedia.

operations and kept the surgical site open to allow continued drainage. The wound however got infected, and with each passing day, Beethoven's condition deteriorated from bad to worse.

By the third week of March, it became apparent that he would not survive. On 24 March *Beethoven signed his last will and testament*, leaving everything he had to his nephew Karl. The same day he received last rites of the Roman Catholic Church. His friends and admirers gathered around him to pay their final respects.

On 26 March Beethoven slipped into unconsciousness, and died, at the age of 56, during a thunderstorm. While others, including Beethoven's brother and some friends, were probably in the house, only his sister-in-law and his friend Anselm Hüttenbrenner were present in the room at the time of his death.

"That day was tragic." French dramatist, novelist, essayist, art historian Romain Rolland writes describing Beethoven's final day,[65]

> *"There were heavy clouds in the sky… around 4 or 5 in the afternoon the murky clouds cast darkness in the entire room.*

Romain Rolland

---

[65] Rolland, Romain: "*Beethoven*", Published by Forgotten Books, 27 September 2018.

Suddenly a terrible storm started, with blizzard and snow... thunder made the room shudder, illuminating it with the cursed reflection of lightning on snow. Beethoven opened his eyes and with a threatening gesture raised his right arm towards the sky with his fist clenched. The expression of his face was horrifying. His hand fell to the ground. His eyes closed. Beethoven was no more."

Three days later, on 29 March 1827 Beethoven's funeral was held at the parish church in Alsergrund and he was buried in the Wahring cemetery, northwest of Vienna. More than 20,000 people attended the funeral. It was the largest the city had ever seen. Theaters were closed, and several artists participated in the funeral procession as torchbearers, including the celebrated composer Johann Nepomuk Hummel, dramatist Franz Grillparzer, and composer and pianist Carl Czerny. Schubert was also a torchbearer in Beethoven's funeral procession.

As one of his ardent admirers, Schubert was shattered by Beethoven's death. It had a profound impact on him and his music. All his life Schubert had idolized Beethoven – he was the musician of his dream. Many of Schubert's works contain homage to Beethoven.

On one occasion, after playing some compositions of his own, Schubert asked a friend if he could ever expect to do anything great in music; and on his friend replying that he had already done something, he said: "*I think so myself sometimes; yet who can hope to do anything after Beethoven?*"

Schubert spent his whole life in Beethoven's shadow. He had none of the ambition or savvy of Beethoven, his senior by 26 years, who took Vienna by storm before Schubert was even born. They lived in the same city for years, but they hardly knew each other. Beethoven was a celebrated performer almost from the day he made his debut in Vienna in 1795, and his compositions were internationally performed and widely published.

Schubert made no secret of his fondness for Beethoven's music. In 1822, he published a set of variations dedicated to Beethoven: *"by his admirer and worshipper, Franz Schubert."*

On March 19, 1827, Schubert visited Beethoven for the only time. Beethoven was very ill and died just a week later; Schubert helped to carry the coffin at the public funeral. A year and a half later, Schubert's own grave was dug in the same cemetery, separated from Beethoven's by just three others. Five days before he died, Schubert wished to hear Beethoven's C-sharp minor string quartet; and Karl Holz, one of the violinists in Ignaz Schuppanzigh's string quartet, who played it for him that week, later described this musical offering in words the music world would never forget: *"The King of Harmony had sent the King of Song a friendly bidding to the crossing."*

On Beethoven's death anniversary, Schubert plays his maiden public concert

Schubert's friends had often suggested to him that he should give a concert of his own. Though it was a difficult task to convince him, his friend Bauernfeld was able to persuade him to give the concert. Schubert began to plan for a benefit concert in the Philharmonic Society hall entirely devoted to his own music, exactly as Beethoven had done on several occasions. At last, on 26 March 1828, the anniversary of Beethoven's death, Schubert gave, for the first time in his career, a public concert of his own works.

The concert was the greatest success of Schubert's career, bringing him a handsome profit of 800 florins; and the penniless Schubert was at last able to buy himself a piano. *"I shall never forget how glorious it was,"* wrote one of Schubert's friends in his diary. *"Enormous applause. Good receipts."* Another friend noted: *"Everyone was lost in a frenzy of admiration and rapture."* And it all happened in spite of the presence of Niccolò Paganini, the legendary Italian violin virtuoso, in Vienna at that time.

Niccolò Paganini: The Devil's Violinist

The salon where the concert was performed was packed, and it was such a great success that a repetition was proposed. But Schubert did not live to carry out this plan; he died barely eight months later. The 26 March 1828 concert was to be his first and last.

The tragedy of Beethoven's death had a profound impact on Schubert. A distinct, fervent,, intellectual imprint akin to that in Beethoven's music is thus discernible in Schubert's last instrumental works especially, in the '*Piano Trio in E-flat major*' (1827), the '*Piano Sonata in C minor*' (1828) --- and, above all, in his majestic "*Symphony No. 9 in C major*", D. 944 -- commonly called the "*Great*".

Symphony No. 9 in C major **('Great')** *(1827)*

> ***"[The symphony] transports us into a world where I cannot recall ever having been before."***
>
> **--Robert Schumann**

In a letter of March 1824 Schubert had written to a friend that he was preparing to compose *'a grand symphony'* (originally listed as Gmunden-Gastein symphony, D 849, in the Deutsch Catalogue). He began work on this 'grand' symphony in the summer of 1825 and continued it over the next two years.

By the spring or summer of 1826 it was completely scored, and in October, Schubert, who was quite unable to pay for a performance, sent it to the Gesellschaft der Musikfreunde ('Society of Friends of Music') in Vienna with a dedication.

At the end of 1826 he received a letter of thanks, accompanied by a gift of one hundred florins, from the *"Gesellschaft der Musikfreunde"* in recognition of his valuable services to further the objects of the Society. The Society also helped in arranging for the copying of the orchestral parts of the symphony. In return for this courtesy, Schubert presented the Society in the latter half of 1827 with the 'grand' symphony he was working on.

In 1828 the Society decided to premiere the symphony, but the orchestra struggled with the length and technical complexity of the new piece and ultimately declared it as "impracticable". Unusually long for a symphony of its time, a typical performance of the new symphony ('Great') takes around 55 minutes.

To overcome the difficulty, Schubert, in its place, offered the Society a shorter work in the same key, his *Symphony No. 6 (Little C Major)*. But unfortunately it could not be performed during his life time. He died only three weeks before that work's premiere on December 14, 1828.[66]

The unperformed symphony perhaps would have vanished if not for the intervention of Robert Schumann. In 1838, ten years after Schubert's death, Schumann visited Vienna where he met with Schubert's brother Ferdinand, who showed him the scores of several of Schubert's unperformed works, including the manuscript of the

---

[66] A recent hypothesis suggests that the symphony may have received its first performance on 12 March 1829 in a 'Concert Spirituel at the Landständischer Saal of the Palais Niederösterreich' in Vienna. The evidence for this hypothesis is, however, slender, and it contradicts contemporary sources which prove that Schubert's Symphony No. 6 (also in C major) was performed at this instance. In 1836 Schubert's brother Ferdinand attempted to perform the final movement alone, yet there is no evidence that a public performance ever took place.[See, Wikipedia]

symphony ('Great') at the *"Society of Friends of Music"*. *"The riches,"* Schumann wrote later, *"that lay here made me tremble with excitement."* The symphony *"transports us into a world where I cannot recall ever having been before."*

Ferdinand Schubert

This is the *"Symphony No. 9 in C major"*, D 944, the final symphony completed by Schubert. It was first published by Breitkopf & Härtel in 1849 as "*Symphonie / C Dur / für großes Orchester*" ('Symphony / C major / for large orchestra)[67] and listed as Symphony No. 8 in the New Schubert Edition. Originally called *"The Great C major"* to distinguish it from his *"Symphony No. 6, the Little C major"*,[68] the subtitle is now usually taken as a reference to the symphony's majesty.[69]

---

[67] DeVoto, Mark (2011). "*Background: Schubert's Great C Major: Biography of a Symphony*". Boydell and Brewer. pp. 1–12.

[68] Huscher, Philip: "*Program Notes: Schubert, Symphony No. 9*" Chicago Symphony Orchestra, 2012.

[69] There continues to be long-standing controversy regarding the numbering of this symphony, with some scholars (usually German speaking) numbering it as Symphony No. 7. The most

'Great' premiered in Leipzig: More than a decade after Schubert's death

An overwhelmed Schumann persuaded Ferdinand to give him a copy of the symphony, the *'Great'*, and took it to Leipzig, where the work was performed publicly for the first time the entire symphony (albeit with some cuts)[70] by Felix Mendelssohn, the famous German composer and conductor, at the concert hall in Leipzig on 21 March 1839. Schumann celebrated the event in the *"Neue Zeitschrift fur Musik"* ('New Journal of Music'), a music magazine, with an article in which he hailed the symphony for its *"heavenly length"*.

Felix Mendelssohn

It, however, still took many years for the symphony to become established because of its technical complexities. After it was performed by Mendelssohn in Leipzig in 1839 with noteworthy success, it was taken up again in the following year in Vienna, but only

---

recent version of the Deutsch catalogue (the standard catalogue of Schubert's works, compiled by Otto Erich Deutsch) lists it as No. 8, while most English-speaking scholars list it as No. 9. {See, Wikipedia]

[70] *"Symphony No. 9 in C Major"*, Written by Betsy Schwarm, Encyclopedia Britannica.

two movements were given, and these were separated by a Donizetti aria![71] Three years later in 1842, the French violinist, conductor, and composer Habeneck attempted to produce this symphony in Paris, but the band rebelled over the first movement, and the same result followed in London, two years later still, in 1844 when Mendelssohn put it in rehearsal for a Philharmonic concert. London, he found orchestras completely unwilling to play it and the violinists collapsed in laughter when rehearsing the second subject of the finale. These things would perhaps seem strange today, but they are historic facts, and help to explain why Schubert, with all his melody and spontaneity, made his way so slowly to popular appreciation. As Dvořák rightly points out: *"he was young, modest, and unknown, and musicians did not hesitate to slight a symphony which they would have felt bound to study, had it borne the name of Beethoven or Mozart"*.[72]

With the passage of time, the picture changed. Now, often considered Schubert's finest composition for orchestra, the *"Great"* is reckoned as one of the most outstanding and innovative compositions in western music. Many musical historians believe Schubert's "*Ninth Symphony*" ('Great') opened the way for other greats like Anton Bruckner and Gustav Mahler.

"Symphony No. 9" ('Great') reveals the deep influence of Beethoven on Schubert. Schubert's symphony is nearly as long as Beethoven's own *Symphony No. 9* and it also draws upon Beethoven's compositional approaches. In his own composition, Beethoven relied much on the works of Joseph Haydn and Mozart, but he gave them broader and freer expression. In his composition of *'Great'*, Schubert follows Beethoven's approach more than that of the earlier masters.

---

[71] An 'aria' in an opera is a set-piece song for a solo singer in which the character expresses an emotion or ideal that doesn't necessarily drive the story forward.

[72] Dvořák, Antonin: *"Franz Schubert"*, (in collaboration with Henry T. Finck), published in The Century Illustrated Monthly Magazine, New York, 1894

Schubert was a neighbour of Beethoven in his home city. Being 27 years younger than Beethoven, he possibly felt the urge to pay homage to Beethoven's gigantic influence, but also – crucially – he had the courage to realise that what he could do as a composer was radically different from what Beethoven could, and then have the gumption to go ahead and do it. Which is why, in the finale of Schubert's Ninth Symphony, the "Great" C Major, there's a quotation from the Beethoven's Ninth. Schubert wrote his own ninth symphony in 1825, a year after Beethoven's had its premiere, which the younger composer also attended. And on one hand, with this quotation from the Ode to Joy theme from Beethoven's epic finale he was explicitly acknowledging his debt to him, but he was also daring to compete with Beethoven's signature reputation as a symphonist.[73]

For *'Great'*, Schumann's words *"heavenly length"* became the piece's most famous description, though some naysayers sometimes had a different view, particularly about the *"heavenly"* part. Like, as late as 1892 George Bernard Shaw, an often perspicacious music critic, complained that *"a more exasperatingly brainless composition was never put on paper."* However, time proved Schubert was simply ahead of his time. Thus, with the passage of time, as listeners became increasingly comfortable with very large-scale compositions, the structural integrity of Schubert's Great Symphony become clearer. In fact, analysis of the *'Great'* Symphony suggests that its elements are manipulated a good deal more tightly than the materials of the "*Unfinished Symphony*", which nobody complained about,—although, of course, the latter was far shorter overall than *'Great'*, being really only half a symphony.[74]

---

[73] Service, Tom: "*Symphony guide: Schubert's Ninth ('the Great')*", The Guardian, 17 Jun 2014.

[74] Keller, James M.: "*Schubert: Symphony in C major, D.944, The Great*", Program Notes, San Francisco Symphony, October 2017. https://shorturl.at/bIJOP

Winterreise ('The Winter Journey') *(1827)*

Though all his life Schubert was a victim of misfortune and unwarranted rejection, he never allowed his frustration and failure to interfere with his creative genius. But as his health condition worsened and he increasingly realized he was approaching death, the streak of gloom that had pervaded his life began to manifest in his compositions. About this time, Schubert composed another masterpiece -- "*Winterreise*" ("The Winter Journey"), D. 911 -- a song cycle for voice and piano, based on a setting of 24 poems by German poet Wilhelm Müller, taken from Müller's collection "*Die Winterreise.*"

Wilhelm Müller

The lyrics of "*Winterreise*" tell the story of a lonely traveller who ventures out into the snow on a journey to rid himself of his lost love. Along the way he experiences a turmoil of different emotions, mostly ranging from despair to greater despair. "*Winterreise*" by Schubert is essentially, therefore, a masterpiece of the Lieder tradition, portraying the emotional and physical journey of a lovelorn wanderer in a desolate winter landscape. Its combination of beautifully crafted music and evocative poetry creates a work of enduring emotional power and artistry. Each song in the cycle represents a stage in the protagonist's emotional journey as he grapples with his unrequited love and sense of alienation. "*Winterreise*" captures the bleak, wintry landscape and the protagonist's emotional turmoil. Schubert's music creates a powerful atmosphere of melancholy, desolation, and resignation. The use of minor keys, slow tempos, and expressive melodies contributes to this mood.

"*Winterreise*" has been celebrated for its innovative use of song form, as it goes beyond traditional strophic[75] (verse-chorus) song structures. It is seen as a bridge between classical and romantic musical styles.

Composed in 1827, "*Winterreise*" is the second of Schubert's two great song cycles on Müller's poems, the earlier one being "*Die schöne Müllerin*" ('The Beautiful Maid of the Mill'). The two song cycles hold a unique place in the history of western classical music.

On 4 March 1827, Schubert had invited a group of friends to his lodgings to sing the first group of songs in "*Winterreise*", but for some compelling reason, he was out when they arrived, and so it had to wait until later in the year, when the full performance was given.

Reflecting on Schubert's life and music, his staunchest friend, Josef von Spaun, writes that Schubert was in a '*gloomy*' mood while composing "*Winterreise*", and even claims that work on these songs hastened the composer's death. About this time, Schubert was suffering more than usual from nausea and headaches, perhaps exacerbated by bouts of heavy drinking;

In the words of poet Johann Mayrhofer, another close friend of the composer, at the time of composition of "'*Winterreise*', Schubert was in a deep melancholic state of mind, and "*life had lost its rosiness and winter was upon him*".

---

[75] Songs that repeat the same basic multi-phrase unit throughout are in strophic form (sometimes abbreviated AAA because the same basic material, A, is repeated), and the basic unit that is repeated is called a strophe . Strophic form is more common in early rock-and-roll (1950s–1960s) than in the 1970s and beyond. [See, Wikipedia]

'Winterreise' was composed in two parts, each containing twelve songs. The first part was composed in February 1827. In September 1827, Schubert spent a short holiday in Graz. On his return, he resumed work on the second part and completed it in October 1827. The two parts were also published separately by Haslinger, the first on 14 January 1828, and the second one on 30 December 1828, shortly after the Schubert's death.

In *'Winterreise'*, Schubert raises the prominence of the pianist at par with the singer. The piano's rhythms constantly express the moods of the poet. The piano expresses the imagery of nature in the poems, the creatures and the objects, the rushing storm, the crying wind, the water under the ice and the singing of the birds.

Tragically, Schubert died in 1828, just one year after composing "Winterreise." After his death, the cycle started to gain prominence as part of his enduring legacy. His close friend, the composer Franz Liszt, played a crucial role in promoting Schubert's music, including "*Winterreise.*"

Schubert's *'Winterreise'* has had a marked influence on several key works, both the original music and text, of the subsequent period. "*Winterreise*" has been interpreted and performed by numerous celebrated singers and pianists over the years. Each interpretation brings a unique perspective to the work, contributing to its continued popularity and exploration of its emotional depths. "*Winterreise*" stands as a significant work within the Romantic era, characterized by its emphasis on emotion, individualism, and the expression of inner experience. The cycle reflects the Romantic fascination with nature, the sublime, and the exploration of deep, often melancholic, emotions.

In 1994 Polish poet Stanislaw Baranczak published poems inspired by Schubert's music in *'Winterreise'*. "*Winterreise*" is now regarded as one of Schubert's most important and profound compositions, often considered a pinnacle of the Lieder tradition. It has a lasting legacy and is celebrated as an exemplary work that bridges the classical and romantic musical periods. It continues to be performed and admired by musicians and audiences worldwide, and remains a testament to the power of music and poetry to convey deep human emotions and experiences.

"*Winterreise*" remains a staple of classical music repertoire, as it continues to be analyzed and discussed by scholars, musicians, and music lovers. The work's enduring popularity underscores its timeless exploration of the human condition.

Piano Trio in E-flat Major (1827)

"spirited, masculine and dramatic" …. "A Trio by Schubert passed across the musical world like some angry comet in the sky".

-- Robert Schumann

In November 1827, Schubert completed one of his last compositions -- *"Piano Trio" in E-flat major'*, D. 929, for piano, violin, and violin cello. It was written within a few weeks for his close friend Josef von Spaun's engagement party, and performed in January 1828, just a few months before he died. The Trio was published by Probst in late 1828, shortly before the composer's death.

Schubert at the pianoforte during a musicale at the home of Josef von Spaun

Schubert's *"Piano Trio in E-flat Major"* is considered one of the great masterpieces of the piano trio repertoire. It is believed to have been written as a result of a commission from the violinist Ignaz Schuppanzigh, a prominent chamber musician of the time. Schubert, who was suffering from severe health issues at the time, poured his emotions into this composition, and it is often seen as a reflection of his inner turmoil.

The trio is in four movements, a common structure for classical chamber music. The opening movement is marked by its lyrical and dramatic themes (Allegro[76]); the second movement is a beautiful and melancholic Andante con moto[77], featuring a poignant melody; the third movement is a lively and playful Scherzo[78]; the final movement, an Allegro moderato[79], is characterized by its joyful and triumphant character.

The trio was performed publicly in March 1828 in Vienna, with Carl Maria von Bocklet on the piano, Ignaz Schuppanzigh playing the violin, and Josef Linke playing cello. The concert was a huge success, and provided a sudden windfall for Schubert, which enabled him to pay off his debts.

The *E-flat Trio*, like many of Schubert's works, gained recognition and acclaim in the years following the composer's death. It was first published in 1836, seven years after Schubert's passing, and became a significant part of the chamber music repertoire. The trio's emotional

---

[76] Performed at a brisk speed.

[77] The tempo of '*andante con moto*' indicates "slowly, but with motion". This direction informs the performer that whilst the music should be slow, it should not be so slow that things grind to a halt.

[78] A '*scherzo*' in western classical music, is a short composition – sometimes a movement from a larger work such as a symphony or a sonata. The precise definition has varied over the years, but scherzo often refers to a movement that replaces the minuet as the third movement in a four-movement work, such as a symphony, sonata, or string quartet. The term can also refer to a fast-moving humorous composition that may or may not be part of a larger work. [See, Wikipedia]

[79] '*Allegro moderato*' in music means "moderately fast", or "fast but not too fast". Since allegro encompasses a tempo range of 120 to 168 beats per minute (BPM), allegro moderato would likely appear somewhere in the middle of that range. [See, Wikipedia]

depth and the combination of Schubert's lyrical melodies with classical forms have made it a beloved and enduring piece.

Schubert's *Piano Trio in E-flat Major* has had a profound influence on subsequent generations of composers and musicians. Its emotional intensity, melodic richness, and harmonic inventiveness have made it a cornerstone of the chamber music repertoire. The trio remains a popular and frequently performed work in the classical music world.

Describing the work as *"spirited, masculine and dramatic"*, Schumann, who was extremely fond of Schubert's music, wrote, "*A Trio by Schubert passed across the musical world like some angry comet in the sky*".

Chapter 8
Schubert's Last Year (1828)

A number of masterpieces mark the last year of Schubert's life. The passionate Schubertian & composer Benjamin Britten, has described the period of 13 months between the completion of *'Winterreise'* in late October 1827 and the composer's death in November 1828 as the most 'miraculous' year in the history of music. Schubert had perhaps sensed that for him time was running out. So in spite of his failing health, he remained absorbed in his work.

It was during this time in March 1828 Schubert produced what is probably his greatest piano duet -- "*Fantasy in F minor*". The same month he also composed the cantata "*Miriams Sieges gesang*" ('Miriam's Victory Song'), D. 942.

In June, Schubert worked on his "*Sixth mass in E-flat major*", D. 950. In August, he composed the collection of songs published together as the "*Schwanengesang*" ('Swan Song'), D. 957. In September and early October, just one month before his death, he composed the "*last three piano sonatas [in C minor, A major, and B-flat major]*", (D. 958, 959 and 960) and his final chamber work – the "*String Quintet*" in C *major*('Cello Quintet'), D. 956.

Fantasia in F minor ('Fantasy') *(1828)*

The "*Fantasia*" in F minor, D. 940, Op. posth. 103 by Schubert, written for piano four hands, is one of his most important piano works. It is a farewell to numerous characters and to all the pretty things he loved.

Schubert composed "Fantasia" in the last year of his life, and dedicated it to his pupil, Caroline Esterhazy, with whom he was in unrequited love.

The Fantasia is divided into four connected movements. It does not adhere to a traditional sonata-allegro or ternary structure but rather flows seamlessly from one section to the next.

Schubert's Fantasia in F minor is notable for its emotional depth and complexity. It is one of his more extended piano compositions and showcases his mastery of harmonic progressions and melodic inventiveness. The piece is often considered a testament to Schubert's genius, written during the last year of his life when he was grappling with illness and personal difficulties.

Musicologist Christopher Gibbs has characterized the work as "*among not only his greatest but his most original*" compositions for piano duet

Schubert began writing the "*Fantasia*" in January 1828 in Vienna. The work was completed in March, and premiered in May, just a few months before his death. Schubert's friend Bauernfeld recorded in his diary on May 9 that a memorable duet was played, by Schubert and Lachner, his aspiring young composer friend, who later became a distinguished conductor. It was published by Diabelli in March 1829. The original manuscript resides at the Austrian National Library.

Franz Paul Lachner

The Fantasia in F minor is a challenging work, both technically and emotionally, and it is highly regarded in the classical piano repertoire. It requires two skilled pianists to perform it effectively, as it demands coordination and communication between the players. It has been recorded by many renowned pianists and remains a staple of the chamber music repertoire.

Schubert's Fantasia in F minor is a remarkable work that reflects his unique Romantic style, marked by rich harmonies, poignant melodies, and deep emotional expression. It is celebrated for its beauty and complexity and continues to be appreciated by musicians and audiences worldwide.

Schubert's Last Sonatas (1828)

The last three piano sonatas, D. 958, 959 and 960 of Franz Schubert were written during the last months of his life. Schubert had been suffering from the effects of syphilis for some time. But despite his illness he was at the peak of his creative spree in the last year of his life. Music publishers were also beginning to show more interest in his works; and for a while Schubert was somewhat free from financial worries.

Up until the very last week of his life, Schubert continued to compose, but thereafter he had to give up. On September 26, 1828 he finished his last piano sonata. Two days later, he played from the sonata trilogy at an evening gathering in Vienna. In a letter dated October 2, 1828 to his publisher Probst, Schubert offered the sonatas amongst his other works for publication. But Probst was not interested in the sonatas, and barely six weeks later, on November 19, Schubert breathed his last.

The following year, his brother Ferdinand sold the sonatas' autograph to Diabelli, who published them a decade later. Schubert had intended the sonatas to be dedicated to Johann Nepomuk Hummel, the illustrious Austrian composer and virtuoso pianist, whom he greatly admired. But by the time the sonatas were published, Hummel was dead, and Diabelli dedicated them to Robert Schumann, the German composer and an influential music critic, who had praised many of Schubert's works in his critical writings.

Johann Nepomuk Hummel

Schubert's last sonatas (Piano Sonata in C minor (D. 958), Piano Sonata in A major (D. 959), and Piano Sonata in B-flat major (D. 960)) represent a departure from his earlier sonatas, showing a maturity and innovation in his composition that was influenced by the works of Beethoven and other late Classical and early Romantic composers.

Schubert's last sonatas are seen as a bridge between the Classical and Romantic eras in music. They display harmonic innovations and structural complexity that were ahead of their time, influencing later composers like Robert Schumann and Franz Liszt. These sonatas are renowned particularly, for their emotional depth, lyrical beauty, and thematic development, showcasing Schubert's gift for melody and his ability to convey profound emotions through his music.

Despite their exclusive composition and brilliance, Schubert's piano sonatas unfortunately did not receive much attention during most of the 19th century. Johannes Brahms, the great German composer and pianist, was, however, fond of Schubert's sonatas and studied them intensely. In the 20th century, the noted Austrian pianist Artur

Schnabel championed the works and played them in recitals. The sonatas are now considered among the most important of the Schubert's masterpieces.

Artur Schnabel

Apart from Artur Schnabel, many other renowned pianists have left their mark with interpretations of Schubert's last sonatas. Some notable performers who have recorded these sonatas include, András Schiff, Mitsuko Uchida, and many others.

Schubert's late sonatas have had a profound impact on the classical music world. They are studied and performed by pianists worldwide and continue to captivate audiences with their emotional depth and complexity. Composers like Johannes Brahms, Robert Schumann, and Franz Liszt were inspired by Schubert's late sonatas in their own compositions.

Schubert's last sonatas represent a pinnacle of his creative output and remain an essential part of the piano repertoire. They are admired for their depth, innovation, and the profound emotions they convey, making them a testament to Schubert's genius and his significant contribution to the development of Romantic music.

Schubert's Final Chamber Music: String Quintet in C major (Cello Quintet) *(1828)*

Schubert's final chamber work, the *"String Quintet in C major"*, D. 956, commonly referred to as the "Cello Quintet"[80] because it is scored for two violins, one viola, and two cellos, was composed in the summer or early autumn of 1828 -- just two months before his death.[81] More than two decades later, in 1850, it was premiered at 'Musikverein', a concert hall in the *Innere Stradt* borough (1st municipal District) of Vienna, the home of the famous Vienna Philharmonic orchestra, and was published three years later It has been acclaimed as "*sublime*" and as possessing "*bottomless pathos*," and is generally regarded as Schubert's finest chamber work as well as one of the greatest compositions in all chamber music. The entire piece typically lasts around 50-60 minutes, making it one of the longest works in the chamber music repertoire.

The quintet wasn't performed publicly during Schubert's lifetime, and it was only discovered and published posthumously. When it was finally performed in the 1850s, it received high praise and quickly became recognized as one of Schubert's greatest compositions.

This quintet has been highly influential in the chamber music genre and has inspired countless composers and performers. Its poignant beauty and emotional depth continue to captivate audiences and musicians alike. The quintet has inspired other composers to write their own chamber music masterpieces. As the String Quintet is a late work of Schubert, it foreshadows elements of the Romantic period. Its harmonic explorations and harmonic modulations influenced later Romantic composers like Johannes Brahms and Richard Wagner. Notably, it was Johannes Brahms who was deeply influenced by Schubert's work when composing his own String Quintet No. 1 in F major, which also features two cellos.

---

[80] This quintet is sometimes referred to as Schubert's "Quintet in C" or "String Quintet.".

[81] Schubert's use of two cellos in the quintet rather than the more common two violas expanded the possibilities for chamber music composition. This innovative scoring gave the work a unique depth and richness of sound, and it inspired other composers to experiment with different instrumentations.

Many other world-class chamber ensembles and musicians have also recorded this quintet. Some of the most famous interpretations include those by the Amadeus Quartet with William Pleeth on cello, the Alban Berg Quartet with Heinrich Schiff on cello, and the Emerson String Quartet with Mstislav Rostropovich on cello.

Schubert's String Quintet in C major is a remarkable work that stands as a testament to his compositional genius and emotional depth. It remains a beloved piece in the chamber music repertoire and is celebrated for its beauty and expressive power.

Schwanengesang ('Swan Song') *(1828)*

"*Schwanengesang*" (Swan song) is the title of a collection of songs written by Schubert toward the end of his life and published posthumously. It is not a single unified song cycle but rather a posthumous collection of 14 songs that were published together in 1829, a few years after Schubert's death. The title "*Schwanengesang*" was not given by Schubert but was the result of the publisher's decision, The collection was so named by its publisher Tobias Haslinger presumably wishing to present it as Schubert's final musical testament to the world. Schwanengesang" was published posthumously in 1829, the year after Schubert's death. Some of the songs were published individually before being collected into a single volume. The collection does not have an official opus number, but the songs within it are individually numbered, starting with D. 957. They are often referred to by their individual D numbers.

'Swan song' contains settings of three poets, Ludwig Rellstab, Heinrich Heine and Johann Gabriel Seidl. It was composed in 1828 and published in 1829 -- just a few months after Schubert's death.

The songs in "*Schwanengesang*" are typically performed by a vocalist (usually a tenor or baritone) accompanied by a pianist. The combination of voice and piano allows for a close interplay between the music and the text. The songs in "*Schwanengesang*" are known for their emotional depth and rich harmonic language. They capture the intense emotional and introspective qualities of Schubert's music, a characteristic of his late works. Some of the most well-known songs from "*Schwanengesang*" include "*Ständchen*" (Serenade), "*Aufenthalt*" (Residence), and "*Der Doppelgänger*" (The Double). These songs have been performed and recorded by many renowned vocalists and pianists.

"*Schwanengesang*" has been admired for its melodic beauty and the way it conveys complex emotions. It is a testament to Schubert's ability to set poetry to music effectively.

On 2 October 1828 Schubert had offered the Heine set of poems to his publisher Probst. It, therefore, seems Schubert initially intended to publish the sets separately. As Probst was not agreeable, it remained unpublished. Later Haslinger collected the songs and published together as a cycle, most possibly for financial reasons, as Schubert's earlier two collections of songs, namely, '*Die schöne Müllerin*' and '*Die Winterreise*', sold very well.

The song '*Die Taubenpost* ('The Pigeon Post')', appended by Haslinger at the end to include all of Schubert's last compositions, is considered to be Schubert's last lied.

Liszt later transcribed these songs for solo piano.

Schubert's Lieder, including those in "*Schwanengesang*," had a significant influence on subsequent composers and the development of the German art song tradition. Composers like Schumann, Brahms, and Wolf were inspired by his work.

"*Schwanengesang*" is considered one of Schubert's late masterpieces and is an essential part of the Lieder repertoire. It reflects the emotional intensity and innovation of his work, and its songs continue to be performed and cherished by singers and musicians around the world.

Symphony No. 10 in D major ('Last Symphony') *(1828)*

In the last weeks of his life, Schubert began to sketch three movements for a new "*Symphony No. 10 in D major*", D. 937A -- but it remained unfinished. Written during the last weeks of the composer's short life, it was only properly identified as late as in the 1970s and is now believed to be his *"Last Symphony"*.[82] Later it was conjecturally completed by the British composer, conductor and author Brian Newbould, that has subsequently been performed, published and recorded.

Brian Newbould

Both Sir Charles Mackerras and Sir Neville Marriner have conducted Newbould's conjectural completions of 'Symphony No. 10' by Franz Schubert.

---

[82] The sketch appears to date from the last weeks of the composer's life, in October–November 1828, and is presumed to be the *"Letzte Symphonie"* ('Last Symphony') mentioned by his friend Eduard von Bauernfeld in an appreciation of Schubert published in the *"Wiener Zeitschrift für Kunst, Literatur Theater und Mode"* ('Viennese magazine for art and literature theater and fashion'), for 13 June 1829. [See, Newbould, Brian: *"Schubert and the Symphony: A New Perspective"*, Toccata Press, 1972]

Sir Charles Mackerras

Sir Neville Marriner

The music of the *'Symphony No. 10'* appears to some extent exploratory and contains unusual elements, notably the hybrid form of the third movement and the highly contrapuntal[83] nature of much of the material. Sketches for the third movement are intermingled with several counterpoint exercises,[84] which suggests that it is related in

---

[83] Contrapuntal music has two or more separate tunes that are played or sung at the same time. [See, Cambridge Dictionary]

[84] In music, 'counterpoint' is the relationship between two or more musical lines (or voices) which are harmonically interdependent yet independent in rhythm and melodic contour. It has been most commonly identified in the European classical tradition, strongly developing during the Renaissance and in much of the common practice period, especially in the Baroque period. The term originates from the Latin punctus contra punctum meaning "point against point", i.e. "note against note". [See, Wikipedia]

some way to the single counterpoint lesson Schubert took from Simon Sechter a few weeks before his death in 1828.

Belgian conductor Pierre Bartholomée viewed Newbould's completion as too respectful and conservative. So, he reharmonized parts of it to fit his idea of Schubert's late style, and gave more development to contrapuntal entries only indicated in the manuscript. He also gave the winds more prominent roles. He also adds the scherzo from the D 708A symphonic fragment[85] as the third movement.[86] In this aspect, Bartholomée's edition is debatable as the fragment seems to have been conceived by Schubert in a three-movement form, with the third movement combining elements of a Scherzo and a Rondo. Additionally, Bartholomée did not respect the instruments available at Schubert's time, when he wrote for chromatic horns and trumpets.[87]

Pierre Bartholomée

---

[85] Schubert's Symphony in D major, D 708A (occasionally numbered as Symphony No. 7, although this number more commonly represents another symphony, D 729), is an unfinished work that survives in an incomplete eleven-page sketch written for piano solo. It is one of Schubert's six unfinished symphonies. It was begun in 1820 or 1821, with initial sketches made for the opening sections of the first, second, and fourth movements, and an almost complete sketch for the third movement. He abandoned this symphony after this initial phase of work and never returned to it, although Schubert would live for another seven years.

[86] Stevenson, Joseph. "*Symphony No. 10 in D major (sketch), D. 936a*". The AllMusic guide. Retrieved 7 September 2013.

[87] Wikipedia

Chapter 9
Schubert's Music: Recognition

Schubert's work received little recognition during his lifetime. Compared to Beethoven, Schubert's longer works that are now considered amongst the finest pieces in western classical music were for decades felt to be rambling or lacking in structure. Unfortunately for Schubert, in spite of his superb music, the operas he composed were either not staged or poorly received by the critics, mostly because of weak libretto. One of them only managed a mere six shows before it was forced to close down.

Like other unknown artists, Schubert also had to suffer the misery of being turned down by publishers. *"I only want works by masters already recognized by the public"*, said the publisher Edition Peters after Schubert's friend, Josef Hüttenbrenner, had tried to get some of his works published. Schubert, therefore, had no choice but to turn to his friends to print his works, but the royalty he could earn was a pittance.

Gesellschaft der Musikfreunde **('Society of Friends of Music in Vienna')**

In 1818, Schubert had applied for membership in the "*Gesellschaft der Musikfreunde*" ('Society of Friends of Music') in Vienna to gain admission as an accompanist, and to have the opportunity to perform his music, especially his lieder (songs) in the evening concerts. But he was rejected on the ground he was "no amateur", although at that time there were professional musicians already among the society's membership. If he had been selected then, Schubert's financial distress perhaps would have ended; and it would have helped him to further his musical career. But it was not to be; because of his humble background and with no one to take up his cause, he had to suffer.

Finally, in 1821 the Society accepted him as a performing member; it helped Schubert to remarkably increase the number of his performances and earn admiration and awe respect of the music lovers. Within a short period, his reputation began to grow steadily, and he became well known among the Viennese citizenry. Some of the members of the Society, most notably Ignaz von Sonnleithner and his son Leopold, had a sizeable influence on the affairs of the society. With their support, and also because of Schubert's growing reputation, his works were included in three major concerts of the Society in 1821.

Schubert was never a commanding or charismatic figure. He had none of the ambition or savvy of Beethoven, his senior by 26 years, who took Vienna by storm before Schubert was even born. Most of Schubert's masterpieces were premiered after his death. During his lifetime, he was perceived more as a good song writer; and this impression persisted for quite some time after his death, To many, he was a kind of cardboard caricature — a bohemian coffee-house composer who jotted down songs, one after another, on the tablecloth or the back of a bill of fare, while the world passed him. In contrast to the all-overshadowing Beethoven, Schubert was rather humble and modest in his demeanor; one who felt more at home in the company of his young friends and preferred to avoid the high and aristocratic circles. But in his creative pursuit, he was invincible -- no less than the very best the world of music has ever witnessed. His compositions seem to have been driven by some divine desire. In his own words, *"I am composing like God, as if it simply had to be done as it has been done"*.

Despite his rare genius, Schubert was overlooked by his contemporary time and remained unappreciated for ages after his demise. Even as late as in 1894, in an influential essay, the British scholar and composer Hubert Parry could still maintain that Schubert had no feeling for *"abstract design, and balance and order,"* and *"no taste for the patient balancing, considering, and rewriting again and again, which was characteristic of Beethoven"* — a verdict that remained unchallenged well into the next century

It was only after Schubert's death when illustrious composers like, Schumann, Liszt, Brahms and Mendelssohn performed his works that his music became famous. Since then, interest in his work increased dramatically over the years. Today, he is indisputably amongst the all-time greats in western classical music – in the same class as Mozart, Beethoven and Brahms -- and is one of the world's most frequently performed composers.

Chapter 10
Schubert & Other Vintage Virtuosi

"Once more, and a thousand times more, Bach, Beethoven, and Schubert are the highest summit in music."

-- Anton Rubinstein [88]

Wolfgang Amadeus Mozart (27 January 1756 – 5 December 1791)

"O, Mozart! Immortal Mozart! what countless impressions of a brighter, better life hast thou stamped upon our souls!"

- Franz Schubert

About five years after Mozart's death, Schubert was born. Since his childhood, Schubert was in love with Mozart's music. "*O, Mozart! Immortal Mozart!*" he wrote, "*what countless impressions of a brighter, better life hast thou stamped upon our souls!*"

Wolfgang Amadeus Mozart (1756-1791) was a prominent figure in the Classical period. His music is characterized by clarity, elegance, and balanced structures. He composed in various forms, including symphonies, operas, chamber music, and piano sonatas. Vocal music played a significant role in Mozart's output, with a special emphasis on opera. His operatic works are known for their beautiful melodies, vocal virtuosity, and dramatic storytelling. Operas like "*Don Giovanni*," "*The Marriage of Figaro*," and "Cosi fan tutte" are among his most famous.

Schubert (1797-1828), on the other hand, is considered a bridge between the Classical and Romantic periods. His early works exhibit

---

[88] Anton Grigoryevich Rubinstein (28 November [O.S. 16 November] 1829 – 20 November [O.S. 8 November] 1894) was a famous Russian pianist, composer and conductor who became a pivotal figure in Russian culture when he founded the Saint Petersburg Conservatory. He was the elder brother of Nikolai Rubinstein, who founded the Moscow Conservatory.

classical traits, but his later compositions, particularly in lieder (art songs), showcase the emotional depth and intense expression characteristic of the Romantic era.

Mozart was a child prodigy who showed remarkable musical talent from an early age. He travelled extensively throughout Europe, gaining recognition for his musical genius. Schubert, too, displayed exceptional musical talent at a young age. However, he lived a relatively modest life and faced financial challenges, relying on the support of friends and family. He had a close circle of friends who appreciated his music, and his works gained more recognition after his death.

Mozart's output was remarkably prolific, with over 600 works to his credit. Some of his most famous works include "*Symphony No. 40*," "*The Magic Flute*," and "*Eine kleine Nachtmusik*" ('A little night music'). Schubert's output was also amazing, particularly given the short life he lived. He composed in almost every genre of his time, including symphonies, operas, concertos, chamber music, and piano music. His most well-known works include "*Symphony No. 8*" ('Unfinished Symphony'), "*Ave Maria*," and his many lieder, such as "*Der Erlkönig*". He composed over 600 lieder, setting poems by various German poets to music. His lieder are known for their emotional depth, intimate piano accompaniments, and ability to convey profound sentiments.

Schubert was enamored of Beethoven. He dreamt of him, adored him all his life and even wished to be buried close to him after his death. But perhaps he had a more proximate kinship to Mozart. Both were gifted with an incredible talent for music; they both had "*the same delicate sense of instrumental coloring, the same spontaneous and irrepressible flow of melody, the same instinctive command of the means of expression, the same versatility in all the branches of their art*", and they both composed some of the greatest melodies in history.[89]

> "*Mozart's mature concerto*", it has been said "*anticipates the coming romantic age while Schubert's youthful symphony is a young man's embrace of it.*"

Both died incredibly young, Mozart at 36 and Schubert at 31. It is noteworthy that they both composed their greatest masterpieces at their respective genre, within a remarkably short span, towards the end of their lives. Mozart's last three symphonies numbered 39, 40 and 41 and Schubert's piano sonatas D. 958, D. 959 and D. 960.[90]

Wolfgang Amadeus Mozart

---

[89] Dvořák, Antonín: "*Franz Schubert*", (in collaboration with Henry T. Finck), published in The Century Illustrated Monthly Magazine, New York, 1894.

[90] The Symphony No. 39, 40 and 41 are the last three symphonies that Mozart composed in rapid succession during the summer of 1788. The Symphony No. 39 was completed on 26 June 1788, No. 40 on 25 July and No. 41 on 10 August, 1788.

Schubert's last three piano sonatas, D 958, 959 and 960, are his last major compositions for solo piano. They were written during the last months of his life, between the spring and autumn of 1828, but were not published until about ten years after his death, in 1838 39.

Both Mozart and Schubert were extravagant; and, sadly enough, both died in penury.

> *"Mozart lived his life and arrived at a kind of late style,"* said Alfred Brendel, the Austrian pianist, poet, and author, *"Schubert, on the contrary, was in the middle of a tremendous development when he died."*

Alfred Brendel

In the words of Brian Newbould: *"Mozart and Beethoven are geniuses, but Schubert is a miracle."*

Ludwig van Beethoven (baptised 17 December 1770 – 26 March 1827)

"Truly, the spark of divine genius resides in this Schubert!"

- Ludwig van Beethoven

All his life, Schubert was an ardent admirer of Beethoven; for him, he was the ultimate in music. It is said that the 17-year-old Schubert sold his books in order to buy a ticket for the first performance of the revised version of Beethoven's opera *"Fidelio"* on 23rd May 1814.

Schubert adored Beethoven who was twenty-seven years older than him. He was simply awed by him -- to the point that he was too timid to even introduce himself to the musical giant when the two passed one another on the streets of Vienna. Once he saw Beethoven across the room in a crowded coffee house, but did not have the courage to approach him.

Schubert had lived for about thirty years in the same town as Beethoven. The lustre of the master obscured Schubert's name, and shut up many of the avenues of success, but it did not prejudice Schubert against Beethoven whom he considered to be so vastly superior.

Ludwig van Beethoven

Though they lived in the same town for such a long time, even then the two composers perhaps never met until just before the death of Beethoven. One possible reason why they did not meet earlier was that Beethoven was not easily accessible. The two were radically different in nature. Schubert's character resembled that of Mozart. He was somewhat naive, impractical, unassuming, easy- going, fond of friends irrespective of their social positions, and would have a gala time over a good glass of wine at a roadside cafe. Beethoven, on the other hand, was aristocratic, selective in his choice and preference, and generally moved in high circles. So probably he knew little of the musical gifts of young Schubert till the two met-- albeit too late in the day.

Beethoven's personal secretary and biographer Schindler, however, has a different story to tell. According to Schindler, Schubert set out in 1822 to present his variations for four hands on a French song in E minor, D. 624, Op. 10, which he had dedicated to Beethoven whom he adored all his life. Though he was accompanied by Diabelli, who acted as the interpreter of his feelings for the deaf Beethoven, Schubert was visibly nervous for his maiden meet with his idol. The courage that kept him up till he came to the house forsook him altogether at the sight of the artist monarch. Beethoven ran through the copy of the variations which were presented to him and lighted on a fault in harmony. He pointed it out gracefully to the young man, adding that it was not '*a deadly sin*'; but, perhaps, owing to this gentle remark, Schubert lost all his bearing, and would not recover himself till he left the house, and was distressed over his own conduct. This was his first and last meeting with Beethoven, for after that he never could muster up the courage to present himself again.

This version of Schindler is, however, at variance with what we learn from Schubert's friend Joseph Hüttenbrenner who states distinctly that a short time after publication of the variations, Schubert gave him his own account of the visit to Beethoven. What Schubert said was that he went to Beethoven's house with the variations, but Beethoven was not at home and he, therefore, gave them to a servant. Since then, he had neither seen nor spoken to Beethoven. Later Schubert was much pleased to hear that Beethoven highly appreciated the variations, and often played them through with his nephew Karl.

In his description of the last days of Beethoven, Schindler writes:

> "*As the disease to which Beethoven succumbed after four months of suffering, made it impossible for him from the very first to exert his intellectual activity, it was necessary to find some amusement suited to him. Hence it came that I put before him a collection of Schubert's songs, about sixty in all, many of*

> *them still in manuscript. The great master who had not known more than five songs of Schubert before, was astonished at their number, and would not believe that Schubert had composed more than 500 already. But if he was surprised at their number, he was filled with the utmost astonishment by their merits."*

For several days Beethoven could not tear himself away from Schubert's musical pieces. Surprised at the number that Schubert had already composed, he asked Schindler *"How can he find time to set such long poems, many of them containing ten others?"* He read them over and over again and cried out several times with joyful enthusiasm. He was so impressed with Schubert's works that he exclaimed: "*Truly, the spark of divine genius resides in this Schubert!*" He also predicted that Schubert "*would make a great sensation in the world,*" He desired to see Schubert's operas and pianoforte pieces, but it was too late as his illness grew so much worse that this wish could not be gratified. But from this time till his death, he often spoke of Schubert, regretting that he had not known him earlier.

During the last moments of Beethoven, Schubert stood with many others for a long while around his deathbed. When Beethoven was told the names of his visitors, he made feeble signs to them with his hands. Of Schubert he said: "*Franz has my soul.*"

On March 26, 1827, Beethoven breathed his last. Schubert was a torchbearer in Beethoven's funeral procession. There were 39 other torchbearers, including the composers Hummel and Czerny; Schubert was dressed in mourning, with a bunch of white roses and lilies fastened to the crepe on his arm.

While returning from the funeral with Lachner and Randhartinger, they stopped at the '*Mehlegrube*', a tavern in the Karntner Strasse ('Carinthian street'), now the 'Hotel Munsch'. There they drank wine solemnly to the memory of Beethoven; Schubert lifted his glass and drank a toast "*To him we have just buried*,", then another "*To him who will be next*" to follow the great master on the long, long, journey to fame. Schubert had little idea that he was drinking to himself. He died only a year and a half later.[91]

Tryst with Carl Maria von Weber (c. 18 November 1786 – 5 June 1826)

"I tell you the first puppies and the first operas should always be drowned."

-- **Carl Maria von Weber**

On October 25, 1823, after the maiden performance of the romantic opera *"Euryanthe"* composed by Weber at the Kärntnertor Theater, Schubert and Carl Weber, the famous German composer, came to a near collision course. They were discussing the opera 'Euryanthe', when young Schubert, in his usual frankness, told Weber that the score in the opera did not contain a single original melody. Weber was visibly displeased and insolently retorted *"Let the fool learn something himself before he criticizes me."* In response, Schubert placed before him the score of *"Alfonso and Estrella"* that he had recently composed. Weber looked through it. Presuming that the score before him was Schubert's first attempt, he scornfully commented: *"I tell you the first puppies and the first operas should always be drowned."*

Weber was wrong for he did not know it was actually Schubert's twelfth dramatic work.

---

[91] Plantinga, Leon: *"Beethoven's Concertos: History, Style, Performance"*, New York: W.W. Norton, 1999.

Carl Maria von Weber

Despite the spat between them, after he became more familiar with Schubert, Weber developed great admiration and appreciation for Schubert's genius and made efforts to get his work produced at the prestigious Dresden theatre of which he was the Director.[92]

Felix Mendelssohn (3 February 1809 – 4 November 1847)

"He [Mendelssohn] was the Mozart of the nineteenth century, the most brilliant musician, the one who most clearly sees through the contradictions of the age and for the first time reconciles them."

-- **Robert Schumann**

Jakob Ludwig Felix Mendelssohn Bartholdy, widely known as Felix Mendelssohn, was a prominent German composer, pianist, organist and conductor of the early Romantic period. His contemporary Robert Schumann, the great German composer, wrote of Mendelssohn that he was "*the Mozart of the nineteenth century, the most brilliant musician, the one who most clearly sees through the contradictions of the age and for the first time reconciles them.*" Mendelssohn had a deep

---

[92] Grove, George Sir. *"Beethoven – Schubert Mendelssohn"*, Read Books, March 15, 2007.

appreciation for the music of Franz Schubert, and played a significant role in reviving and promoting Schubert's music.

Mendelssohn was instrumental in popularizing Schubert's work in the 19th century when Schubert's music was still relatively unknown. Schubert had tragically passed away in 1828 at a young age of 31. As a result, his music did not enjoy widespread recognition during his lifetime, and much of it remained unpublished or unknown. Mendelssohn, himself a highly regarded composer and conductor, played a crucial role in rediscovering Schubert's works. He first encountered Schubert's music during a visit to Vienna in 1822 and was deeply impressed. He discovered and championed some of Schubert's important compositions, especially his symphonies and chamber music. Here are a few notable contributions Mendelssohn made to Schubert's legacy:

Felix Mendelssohn

Rediscovery of the "Great" C Major Symphony: Mendelssohn conducted the first performance of Schubert's Symphony No. 9 in C Major, (popularly known as the "*Great*"), in Leipzig in 1839, a decade after Schubert's death. This performance played a crucial role in establishing the work's reputation as one of Schubert's greatest masterpieces.

Publication of Schubert's Lieder: Schubert's lieder (art songs) are among his most celebrated works. Mendelssohn's efforts to popularize Schubert's lieder were notable. He included Schubert's songs in his concert programs and published several collections of Schubert's lieder, making them more accessible to singers and audiences. Mendelssohn's arrangements and performances of Schubert's lieder helped establish them as an essential part of the Romantic song repertoire.

Promotion of Schubert's Chamber Music: Mendelssohn also promoted Schubert's chamber music, including his piano quintet in A Major (known as the "*Trout*" Quintet), which Mendelssohn performed and popularized.

Publishing and Preservation: Mendelssohn played a pivotal role in getting Schubert's compositions published. He arranged for the publication of several of Schubert's instrumental and vocal works, ensuring that they would not be lost to history. By publishing these works, Mendelssohn contributed to the preservation and dissemination of Schubert's music.

Influence on Later Composers: Mendelssohn's advocacy for Schubert's music influenced other composers and musicians of his time. Composers such as Robert Schumann and Franz Liszt were also inspired by Schubert's works, in part due to Mendelssohn's efforts. This ripple effect further contributed to Schubert's posthumous recognition.

Mendelssohn's contribution in popularizing Schubert's music was, therefore, multi-faceted. He introduced Schubert's compositions to a wider audience through his performances, publications, and arrangements. Mendelssohn's enthusiasm for Schubert's music greatly helped in the growing recognition and appreciation of Schubert's work in the 19th century and elevate it to the status of a cherished and essential part of the Romantic musical canon, ensuring that Schubert's genius would be recognized and celebrated for generations to come.

Robert Schumann (8 June 1810 – 29 July 1856)

> *"Schubert's pencil was dipped in moonbeams and in the flame of the sun!"*
>
> **- Robert Schumann**

The great German composer, Robert Schumann, was an ardent enthusiast for Schubert. He had been one of the first to recognize Schubert's genius. At 18, he wrote him a fan letter, but unaccountably did not mail it. He is also said to have *"cried all night"* when, at the age of 18, he heard of Schubert's death.

Robert Schumann

In 1838, nearly a decade after Schubert's death, Schumann visited Vienna and met Schubert's brother, Ferdinand, who still held the manuscripts for many works of Schubert, notwithstanding the fact that he had by then sold the majority to Diabelli and Co. Included in the manuscripts he still held were the symphonies like the *"Great"* (Symphony No. 9 in C major), the masses, the operas, etc. Schumann helped Ferdinand to find publishers for these works, and most importantly, his enthusiasm for the *"Great"* led to its premiere in Leipzig under Mendelssohn.

After his discovery of the 'Great', Schumann said that anyone unacquainted with this work *"knows very little about Schubert."* But ironically he himself did not have the luck to know all of Schubert's music, as many more discoveries were to follow. Schumann died on 29 July 1856 and, therefore, he failed to witness the perhaps most impressive find of all — the two movements of the *"Unfinished Symphony"* -- that was performed for the first time in 1865.

In the words of Schumann, "*Schubert's pencil was dipped in moonbeams and in the flame of the sun!*"

Comedy of errors

Interestingly, Schumann has often been confused with Schubert. One such instance of confusion occurred in 1956 when East Germany erroneously issued a pair of postage stamps featuring Schumann's picture against an open score that featured Schubert's music. The stamps were soon replaced by a pair featuring music written by Schumann.

The East Germany 1956 Schumann/Schubert error: Schubert's music is on the top stamp, and Schumann's on the bottom

Franz Liszt (22 October 1811 – 31 July 1886)

"...the most poetic musician who ever lived"

- Franz Liszt

During his 1838 visit in Vienna, Franz Liszt, the renowned Hungarian composer, became virtually absorbed in Schubert's lieder between the years of 1833 and 1845. Explaining what moved him to his intense preoccupation with Schubert's music, Liszt wrote:

> *"I heard in the salons, with vivid pleasure and sentimentality bringing tears to my eyes, an artistic friend, the Baron von Schönstein, present Schubert's lieder. The French translation renders only a very incomplete sense of how this mostly-very-lovely poetry connects to the music of Schubert, ... The German language is so admirable in the area of sentimentality, perhaps only a German is capable of comprehending the naiveté and fantastic aspects of so many of these compositions, their capricious appeal, their melancholy letting-go."*

Franz Liszt

In the words of Liszt, Schubert was *"...the most poetic musician who ever lived"*.

Wilhelm Richard Wagner (22 May 1813 – 13 February 1883)

"Music is the inarticulate speech of the heart, which cannot be compressed into words, because it is infinite."

- Richard Wagner

Richard Wagner, the famous German composer, theatre director, polemicist, and conductor who is chiefly known for his operas (or, as some of his mature works were later known, "music dramas"), was deeply influenced by Schubert's Lieder, in the matching of music to words. And Schubert's harmonies and modulations also greatly inspired Wagner's creations.

Wagner's early compositions, such as his early operas and some orchestral works, show the influence of Schubert. These early works exhibit a more conventional and classical style compared to his later groundbreaking operas. As Wagner developed his unique voice, he moved away from the Schubertian influence, but the impact of Schubert's craftsmanship can still be detected in his early works.

Richard Wagner

Schubert was renowned for his contributions to the genre of Lieder. His ability to convey complex emotions and vivid storytelling through music left a lasting impact on the Romantic composers who followed, including Wagner. Wagner himself composed Lieder early in his career, and Schubert's mastery of this genre inspired him to explore vocal music more deeply.

Schubert was also unusually gifted for crafting beautiful and expressive melodies in his compositions. His ability to create memorable and emotionally charged tunes influenced Wagner, who also sought to create melodies that could convey profound emotional depth. Wagner's operas, like "*Tristan und Isolde*," are known for their lush and expressive melodic lines, and this may be attributed, in part, to Schubert's influence.

Both Schubert and Wagner were known for their innovative harmonic language. Schubert often used chromaticism (the use of notes outside of the key) to create tension and emotional depth in his music. Wagner took this harmonic experimentation further, pushing the boundaries of tonality and chromaticism in his operas. While Wagner's harmonic language is more complex, Schubert's exploration of chromaticism served as a precursor to Wagner's more radical harmonic ideas.

Both Schubert and Wagner were influenced by literature and poetry. Schubert often set the works of famous poets to music in his Lieder, while Wagner drew inspiration from epic sagas and mythology. This shared interest in storytelling through music, whether in miniature form (Lieder) or grand opera, reflects a commonality in their artistic approach.

Schubert's influence on Wagner can thus be seen in their shared interest in expressive melody, harmonic innovation, storytelling through music, and the early compositions of Wagner. It must, therefore, be admitted that while Wagner ultimately developed his distinctive style and pushed the boundaries of classical music, Schubert's contributions as such undoubtedly left a mark on the musical landscape of the 19th century and influenced subsequent generations of composers, including Richard Wagner.

Johannes Brahms (7 May 1833 – 3 April 1897)

"My love for Schubert is a very serious one, probably just because it is not a fleeting fancy. ... To me he is a like a child of the gods, who plays with Jupiter's thunders, albeit also occasionally handling it oddly..."

--- Johannes Brahms

It would be no exaggeration to state that the famous German composer, pianist, and conductor Johannes Brahms was among the most prominent composers of the XIX century in Europe.

Brahms response to influence was always selective, and he came late to Schubert, who was the last great source of influence he discovered. But as he told a friend in the early 1860s, his love for Schubert was lasting and intense, and in a real sense Brahms celebrated Schubert for the rest of his life.

Brahms included Schubert's *Ava Maria* in his second public concert. Yet his youthful friend Louise Japha reported, of the late 1840s and/or the very early 1850s, that "Bach and Beethoven were his chief gods". In 1853, Brahms met Schubert enthusiasts like Joachim and Schumann and heard the Great C major at Leipzig, of which he wrote: *"Little has ever delighted me so much"* His library holdings, noted around December 1854, show Schubert squeezed in with just six listings while other major composers have a page to themselves. It was during the mid-1850s that Brahms began to accord Schubert as great a place in his musical environment as Bach and Beethoven. He played a C major march and the *Rondo brillant* [93] (with Joachim) in concerts in 1855

---

[93] *rondo*: a musical form in which a certain section returns repeatedly, interspersed with other sections: ABACA is a typical structure or ABACABA; *brillante*: brilliantly, with sparkle (See, *"Musical Terminology Glossary"* by Wikipedia).
https://www.translationdirectory.com/glossaries/glossary307.php

and 1856, and the *"Trout"* Quintet, piano trios and violin sonatas at Detmold.[94]

Johannes Brahms

After his first visit to Vienna, Brahms wrote to his friend Schubring in uniquely poetic terms. Though normally a factual, personal and somewhat laconic correspondent, he wrote as follows:

> *"My love for Schubert is a very serious one, probably just because it is not a fleeting fancy. Where is genius like his, which soars aloft so boldly and surely, where we then see the first few enthroned? To me he is a like a child of the gods, who plays with Jupiter's thunders, albeit also occasionally handling it oddly. But he plays in such a region, at a height to which others are far short of raising themselves... I hope now we shall presently be able to chat about this loved one of the gods."*

Unlike Schumann's, Brahms's attachment to Schubert came with maturity. He edited a great number of Schubert's works, and was

---

[94] Pascall, Robert: *"Brahms & Schubert"*, The Musical Times, Vol. 124, No. 1683 (May, 1983), pp. 286-291.

moved by them to follow-up with his own versions of same. For example:

- (i) After accompanying a singer on Schubert's *Die schone Mullerin* and being gifted with a copy of Schubert's complete Lieder, he immediately set to work on his own song-cycle, *Magelone-Romanzen*, Op. 33.
- (ii) His editorial work on Schubert's Mass in E-flat directly influenced his own great German Requiem.
- (iii) After editing 12 Landler [95] by Schubert, Brahms composed his Waltzes Op.39, dubbing them, *"two books of innocent waltzes in Schubertian form."*

In fact, a number of Brahms' most popular and lucrative compositions found their inspiration in Schubert, as Brahms freely admitted, like, the *Liebeslieder Walzer* (Love songs waltz), the waltzes for piano, and of course his various collections of Lieder.

Antonín Leopold Dvořák (8 September 1841 – 1 May 1904)

"Schubert's chamber music, especially his string quartets and his trios for pianoforte, violin, and violoncello, must be ranked among the very best of their kind in all musical literature. Of the quartets, the one in D minor is, in my opinion, the most original and important, the one in A minor the most fascinating. Schubert does not try to give his chamber music an orchestral character, yet he attains a marvelous variety of beautiful tonal effects.

-- Antonín Dvořák

The famous Czech composer Antonin Dvořák had been an admirer of Wagner's music since 1857. But from 1873 on, Dvořák's style was "*moving steadily in the direction of classical models*". In 1894, three years prior to the centennial of Schubert's birth, Dvořák wrote an

---

[95] *Landler* is an Austrian and southern German folk dance in moderately slow triple meter, antecedent to the waltz. In fact the Ländler is a homely waltz, and only differs from the waltz in being danced more slowly. Like most early dances, it occasionally has a vocal accompaniment.

article in which he said the composers of the past he admired most were Bach, Mozart, Beethoven and Schubert. As the article was specifically on Schubert, it seems Dvořák had a special liking and inclination toward Schubert.[96]

Antonin Dvorak

Dvorak, it is said, kept Schubert's Impromptus[97] lying on his piano at all times, for his own and his children's use.

---

[96] See, The Century Illustrated Monthly Magazine, Vol. XLVIII, No. 3 (July 1894), pp. 341–46).

[97] An impromptu is a free-form musical composition intended to produce the illusion of spontaneous improvisation. In keeping with this fundamental premise, there is no particular form associated with the impromptu, although ternary and rondo schemes are common. The style of the music is similar to that of other compositions of the period, with such designations as fantasie, caprice, and bagatelle. [See, Encyclopedia Britannica]

Chapter 11
Schubert: The man within

Portraits of Schubert made during his lifetime are rare. In the first edition of his famous *"A Dictionary of Music and Musicians"*, Sir George Grove wrote:[98]

> *"Schubert was not sufficiently important during his lifetime to attract the attention of painters, and although he had more than one artist in his circle, there are but three portraits of him known."* These include first, *"a poor stiff head by Leopold Kupelweiser, full face, taken on July 10, 1821, photographed by Mietke and Wawra of Vienna"*, second, *"a ... half-length, 3-quarter-face, in water colours, by W. A. Rieder, taken in 1825, and now in possession of Dr. Granitsch of Vienna. A replica by the artist, dated 1840, is now in the Musik-Verein"* and lastly, *"the bust on [Schubert's] tomb, which gives a very prosaic version of his features."*

Schubert was by no means a dandy, but he liked colourful clothes and often appeared in a green coat with white pantaloons.

Little mushroom

Schubert was quiet, shy, diminutive (the military rejected him because he was barely 5 feet tall), pudgy, and unkempt in appearance, *"looking not like a god of music but like a harried Viennese clerk with a head-cold"*. His diminutive frame – with his little overweight – earned him the sobriquet '*Schwammerl*' ("little mushroom"). His other nickname was '*Kanevas*'; apparently, he always asked of new acquaintances, '*Kanner was?*' (What can he do?).

---

[98] Grove, Sir George: *"A Dictionary of Music and Musicians"*, Wiki source, p. 371. https://en.wikisource.org/wiki/Page:A_Dictionary_of_Music_and_Musicians_vol_3.djvu/371

He was not quite articulate. In fact, he suffered from a stammer and walked with a shuffle. Because of poor eyesight, he wore gold-rimmed glasses almost all his life and frequently slept in them. His friend Spaun says that Schubert sometimes passed the night at his house and that even during sleep he would keep his spectacles on his nose.

Like many other composers, Schubert liked to drink. There are descriptions of Schubert having "*drunk too much*" on numerous occasions, and smelling heavily of tobacco. One of his friends, Wilhelm von Chézy, noted that "*when the juice of the vine glowed within him, he did not bluster… but liked to withdraw into a corner and give himself contentedly to silent rage*".

Schubert suffered bouts of depression – '*as if pursued*', says his friend Eduard von Bauernfeld, "*by a black-winged demon of sorrow and melancholy*" – disappearing from his circle for long periods and that would often be most astonishingly productive.

Eduard von Bauernfeld

In 1863, the bodies of both Beethoven and Schubert were exhumed and their graves were moved from Wahring to the Vienna Central Cemetery. It was then noticed that Beethoven's skull was thick, with a strong jawbone; Schubert's cranium, on the other hand, was possessed of an almost feminine fineness of construction.

Bohemian

Schubert badly needed a job, but he was bohemian in nature and averse to a regimented lifestyle. He craved for a relaxed environment for work and little would he agree to subject himself to any rules or regulations.

In 1822, Count Dietrichstein, the Director of music to the Imperial Court and one of Schubert's patrons and well-wishers, offered him a post as organist to the Court Chapel, but, like Beethoven, it was not possible for Schubert to undertake any duties requiring strict attendance.

Not only bohemian, but he was stubborn too when it came to his music -- and it often stood in the way of his getting any regular employment. This was apparent when another opportunity of getting a stable income arrived for him during the autumn of 1827.

In 1827, following the removal of the German pianist and composer Karl August Krebs from the conductorship of the court-theatre to Hamburg, Vogl requested Duport, the administrator of the theatre, to engage his friend in his place. Duport was agreeable to consider depending on Schubert's success in composing some scenes for the stage. Madame [Nanette] Schechner, who was to play the lead role and whose voice at that time was on the wane, at the pianoforte rehearsals, objected to some passages, perhaps in her air, and wanted the composer to alter them. But Schubert was not agreeable. The same thing happened at the first orchestral rehearsal when it also became evident that the accompaniments were too noisy for the voice. Still, Schubert would not relent. At the full-band rehearsal, Schechner broke down and refused to sing any more. Duport then stepped in and requested Schubert to alter the music. But Schubert flatly refused, and declared, "I will alter nothing," took up his score and left the house. And with it, the question of his conductorship also came to an end.

Schubert lived a Bohemian life. But he was extremely diligent and disciplined in his creative work. He would rise early in the morning and regularly set to work until about 2 or 3 in the afternoon. "I compose every morning", he would often say, "and when one piece is done, I begin another." Moreover, while he remained absorbed in his musical studies, if an idea seized him, eye-witnesses could guess it from his flashing eyes and altered tone of voice. Schubert, who otherwise was somewhat casual in most worldly matters, would then be an entirely different persona and would at once seek to perpetuate and fix on paper the full treasures of his musical fancies. This was in sharp contrast with his proclivity to be unpunctual at rehearsals, or at times to refuse offers that deprived him of being the master of his time.

Lacked sense of pound, shilling and pence

Schubert had no business sense; he sold the copyright of several of his masterpieces to his publishers for a song. To make matters worse, he had a profligate lifestyle.

Singerstraße 28: The restaurant at this address - "Zu den drei Hacken" ('To The Three Hoes') is where Schubert used to eat, drink and presumably compose his music

Bauernfeld recalls Schubert's bohemian attitude to finances, recklessly spending on friends and drinks if he had any money with him. Once smitten with the Italian violin virtuoso '*Paganini*' fever, he wrote to his friend Hüttenbrenner, "*I have heard an angel sing*". He had taken Bauernfeld to hear the violinist, insisting on paying for his ticket. When his friend protested, Schubert retorted that he had '*piles of money*' and so not to bother.

No wonder, George Bernard Shaw called Schubert "*charming but brainless*".

Chapter 12
Schubert: Love & Romance

Therese Grob

Schubert never married.

In 1814, he had met a young soprano named Therese Grob, daughter of a local silk manufacturer, and wrote several of his liturgical works for her; she was also a soloist in the premiere of his Mass.

Schubert's friend, Holzapfel, writes, Therese was *"no beauty, but shapely, rather plump, with a fresh round little face of a child."* Schubert confessed to Anselm Hüttenbrenner that he had loved her *"very deeply."* *"She was not pretty"*, he said, *"and was pock-marked, but 'good to the heart'."*

Therese Grob

Schubert wanted to marry Therese, but was prevented by the marriage-consent law of 1815 that required an aspiring bridegroom to show he had the means to support a family. Later, Therese married a baker. Poor Schubert told his friend this had greatly pained him and that he *"loved her still,"* but added philosophically *"as a matter of fact, she was not destined for me."*

Schubert composed a number of songs for Therese. Later he sent her brother Heinrich a collection of his songs that the family preserved with them till the twentieth century.

Caroline Esterhazy: Unrequited love

"Schubert seems to be in love for real with Countess E. I like that. He gives her lessons." A single line in his friend Eduard von Bauernfeld's diary bares it all.

Schubert was indeed in love with his piano student Caroline Esterhazy de Galantha.

In 1818 summer, Schubert started giving private music lessons to Countess Caroline Esterhazy and her elder sister Marie at Zseliz— presently called Zeliezovce, a small market town roughly 200 kilometers distant from Vienna --- where the Esterházy family had their summer residence. It is believed that the young Schubert, barely 21-year-old then, soon suffered an unrequited love towards Caroline, but because of the difference in their social and economic status, anything more than a platonic romance was impossible. The son of a parish schoolmaster, a notoriously broken composer prone to drinking, was not deemed a suitable match for a noblewoman. Not in Vienna, not at the beginning of the 19th century.

In spite of the difference in their social and economic status, Schubert was in love with Caroline. As Bauernfeld wrote about him in a letter to a friend:[99]

> "He was, in fact, head over heels in love with ... Countess Esterházy [...]. In addition to his lessons there, he also visited the Count's home, from time to time, under the aegis of his patron, the singer Vogl. [...] On such occasions Schubert was quite content to take a back seat, to remain quietly by the side

---
[99] Newbould, Brian: *"Schubert Studies"*, Routledge. 16 June 2017.

> *of his adored pupil, and to thrust love's arrow ever deeper into his heart. [...] Countess Caroline may be looked upon as his visible, beneficent muse, as the Leonore of this musical Tasso."*

The young composer's feeling towards his pupil is also beautifully portrayed in the following verse penned by Bauernfeld, which reflects Schubert's unrequited sentiments:

> *"In love with a Countess of youthful grace,*
>
> *—A pupil of Galt's; in desperate case*
>
> *Young Schubert surrenders himself to another,*
>
> *And fain would avoid such affectionate pother."*

In May 1824, Schubert returned to Zseliz for a second time and spent the summer at the castle of the Esterházy family. Schubert stayed in one of the guest rooms in the main house and dined with the family.

Countess Caroline had by this time grown into a beautiful woman. Count Esterházy's friend Karl von Schönstein writes in his later reminiscences:

> *"a poetic flame sprang up in Schubert's heart for Caroline. This flame continued to burn until his death."* According to Schönstein, *"Caroline had the greatest regard for him and for his talent but she did not return his love, although she surely must have been aware of his feelings."*

"These lines should not tempt you to believe that I am not well or not in an optimistic mood", Schubert wrote in a letter to his brother Ferdinand in July 1824 while he stayed at Caroline's place, *"Much to the contrary. The happy times when everything seemed to be surrounded by a youthful glory are obviously gone, but I resign myself to the miserable reality that I try to embellish through my fantasy..."*

Caroline, it is believed, once complained that Schubert dedicated no work to her, to which her teacher replied: *"What's the point? Everything is dedicated to you anyway."*

Caroline Esterhazy

During the spring of 1828, Schubert wrote "*Fantasia*" in F minor, D. 940 -- a beautiful piano piece for four hands that forces the pianists to cross arms – with the remote possibility of touching each other. As an expression of his love, Schubert dedicated to Caroline the mellifluous "*Fantasia*" in March 1828 -- a few months before his death. It was published posthumously the following year.

Schubert and Caroline Esterhazy

'*Fantasia*' combines in it both Joy and sadness -- violent emotions and a tender sensuality -- and its tonality is characterized by a deep melancholy, seemingly craving for death. As countless critics and pianists have observed, *"it is hardly fanciful to hear in the yearning central love duet an idealized expression of a relationship which social differences alone made impossible."* The duet was played by Schubert and Franz Lachner in May, 1828.

A number of films have fictionalized Caroline's relationship with Schubert, including '*Gently My Songs Entreat*' (1933), '*Unfinished Symphony*' (1934) and '*Symphony of Love*' (1954). The countess is also a main character in the French novella '*Un été à quatre mains*' ('A summer with four hands').[100]

Schubert had many friends. But still, he was a loner. And his loneliness longed for expression through his music. His love was unrequited. Little did he know that when you give someone your whole heart and she doesn't want it, you cannot take it back. It is gone forever.

'*Love may have the longest arms, but it can still fall short of an embrace.*'[101]

---

[100] Duncan, Edmondstoune, "*Schubert*", J.M. Dent & Company, 1905, p. 99.
[101] McCafferty, Megan: "*Charmed Thirds*", Broadway Books, April 11, 2006.

Chapter 13
Sex life of Franz Schubert

And now we would step into a forbidden territory.

Many biographers are of the view, and Plutarch, the famous Greek biographer, and essayist, is one of them, that *"it is difficult, or rather impossible, to represent a man's life as entirely spotless and free from blame*; and, therefore, *"we should use the best chapters in it to build up the most complete picture and regard this as the true likeness"*[102]

Frankly speaking, Plutarch is no exception. Many people who love music are also of the opinion that it is both vulgar and pointless to pry into the lives of the great composers. As brilliantly articulated by Donal Henahan, the renowned American music critic and journalist and the winner of the Pulitzer Prize for Criticism in 1986, in 'The New York Times' on August 27, 1989, the proponents of this view strongly feel:[103]

> *"Who cares if Wagner was a deadbeat, that Mozart used foul language, that Beethoven tried to sell scores to different publishers simultaneously, that Chopin loved a woman who dressed like a man and smoked cigars? The music they left us is all that counts. If it were to be discovered tomorrow that Rossini liked to tie up cats and pull out their whiskers one by one, would the reputation of "The Barber of Seville" be much affected? No. Genuine art seeks to shed itself of its creator, ideally in time achieving anonymity of the sort enjoyed by the authors of the "Iliad" or the Egyptian 'Book of the Dead'. ... Art is an insoluble enigma, an unsolicited gift of the gods*

---

[102] See Plutarch, *'The Life of Cimon'* [Plutarch: "*Six of Plutarch's Greek Lives: Cimon. Pericles, with the Funeral Oration of Pericles*", Sagwan Press, 23 August 2015.

[103] Henahan Donal: "*Music View: The Dark Side of Schubert*", published in 'The New York Times', August 27, 1989, The New York Times Archives.

mysteriously funneled through its nominal author. Stravinsky expressed that Platonic ideal well when he said, "I am the vessel through which 'Le Sacre' passed."

Donal Henahan

The attitude of the modern day biographers has, however, changed a lot. A glimpse into the private life of a person of eminence is no longer a taboo. Rather it is now considered essential for proper appreciation of one's creative work. Psychobiography is, therefore, a new genre that is receiving increasing attention in literature for comprehensive assessment of a creative genius and his work.

In the changed perspective, therefore, , it is no wonder that for a rare genius like Schubert, the musicologists as well as his biographers would be curious to ascertain whether the composer was an enthusiastic homosexual or, if his sexuality had something to do with his feverishly prolific output. His drastic swings of mood and his tragic death at age 31are, therefore, all matters of immense importance from a researcher's point of view, and to this, we may now turn.

Schubert: The Dark side of his life

Schubert's romantic and sex life has long fascinated posterity, and there have been treatises on his possible homosexuality.

It is by now fairly well established that Schubert had contracted venereal disease – syphilis -- at an early age and had become critically ill for which he had to be hospitalized in 1823. Though the exact cause of his death is still a mystery, there are many who believe that it ultimately caused his death; and by the time he died, he had developed tertiary stage of syphilis. Nevertheless, less than a week after Schubert's death, the Austrian dramatist and poet Josef von Zedlitz wrote in the *"Wiener Zeitschrift für Kunst"* ('Vienna Journal of Art') that Schubert's *"private life was absolutely honourable and worthy, as is always the case with every true artist"*. Although less naive, the obituaries published by Sonnleithner, Spaun and Bauernfeld also glossed over aspects of Schubert's life with which they must have been acquainted. Only his poet friend Mayrhofer acknowledged in his notice that Schubert *"had long been seriously ill, had gone through disheartening experiences, and life for him had shed its rosy colour"*.

But, over the years, extensive research by musicologists and biographers into his private life has brought to the fore many startling facts about the composer's sexual orientation and it has opened up new vistas for a better appreciation of 'Schubert' the man-- his personality and his extra-ordinary music.

In a letter to Josef von Spaun dated 27 November 1825, Anton Ottenwalt was perhaps the first amongst Schubert's friends to observe that Schubert was subject to the *"passions of an eagerly burning sensuality"*. Four years later, Johann Mayrhofer also discreetly echoed the same note when he wrote that Schubert's character *"was a mixture of tenderness and coarseness, sensuality band candor, sociability and melancholy"*.

About three decades later, in 1857, the Russian author, Alexander Dmitryevich Ulybyshev, known for his biography of Wolfgang Amadeus Mozart, noted in his monograph on Beethoven that Schubert had been *"enslaved by passions mauvaises"* ('bad passions'). In the same year, the Schubert's friend and dramatist Eduard von Bauernfeld explained to Ferdinand Luib, the Austrian music critic who later wrote biography of the composer, that *"Schubert had, so to speak, double nature,[...]---- inwardly a poet and outwardly a kind of hedonist"*.

From his childhood acquaintance Josef Kenner's account too, a similar picture emerges. In a letter written in 1858, Kenner observed that Schubert's *"body, strong as it was, succumbed to the cleavage in his – souls --- as I would put it, of which one pressed heavenwards, and the other bathed in slime."* In a subsequent letter, he added, *"Anyone who knew Schubert knows how he was made of two natures, foreign to each other, how powerfully the craving for pleasure dragged his soul to the cesspool of slime"*.

Josef Kenner

Several of Schubert's biographers have drawn from such testimonies the inference that Schubert had a vigorous, clandestine sexual life, and that he probably patronized prostitutes too with disastrous results. Consequently, he contracted syphilis --- that led to his hospitalization sometime in 1823 and to a painful convalescence lingering until 1825 or even 1826. Schubert's intimate friend Franz von Schober, though he himself was no saint, blamed the young composer's illness to *"excessively indulgent sensual living and its consequences"*. Reflecting on the young composer's private life, the German writer, novelist and journalist Wilhelm von Chezy echoed the same sentiments when he wrote: *"Schubert, with his liking for the pleasures of life, had strayed into those wrong paths which generally admit of no return, at least of no healthy one."*

Twenty five years Schubert's senior, the renowned Austrian composer and conductor Ignaz Franz von Mosel met Schubert at the Viennese poet Matthäus von Collin's place around 1820. In his memoirs, Spaun later recalled that, upon hearing Vogl sing some of Schubert's songs, Mosel declared Schubert to be '*by no means just a prolific inventor of melodies, but a thorough musician*'. On 28 February 1823 Schubert wrote a letter to Mosel with which he enclosed the overture and third act of his new opera '*Alfonso und Estrella', which he had just completed and sought his opinion regarding the new composition. Schubert, in his letter, also* asked if Mosel might write him a letter of recommendation to Carl Maria von Weber in Dresden, where Schubert was trying to present a performance. It is significant to note that in the opening sentence of this letter, there is a mention of a development that altered Schubert's life permanently: "*Kindly forgive me if I am compelled to inconvenience you with another letter so soon, but the circumstances of my health still forbid me to leave the house*". Although Schubert remained circumspect about the nature of his malady, the scattered references to its symptoms during his lifetime suggest that it was almost certainly the venereal disease syphilis.

Ignaz Franz von Mosel

Syphilis was common in Europe throughout the 19th century afflicting as many as one in every five inhabitants in some cities --- prevalent amongst those practising a promiscuous lifestyle. That such a lifestyle led to Schubert's illness is now evident from the accounts of those who knew him personally. But the fact that Schubert's nature contained a strong element of sexual excess was long ignored or concealed by his biographers. Though many of the relevant documents in this regard were known to his biographers way back in the 1850s, it was only in the late 1980s that scholars brought the contradictions in the composer's personality out into the open, and since then many sensational revelations about the dark side of Schubert's life have constantly engaged the attention of the musicologists and researchers.

Schubert – Was he a gay?

Memoirists paying tribute to Schubert after his death testified that he was the classic *"confirmed bachelor"*. Schubert's close associate Anselm Hüttenbrenner had declared that Schubert had *"an overruling antipathy to the daughters of Eve"*. In fact, it troubled him that Schubert was *"cold and unforthcoming toward the fair sex at parties,"* so that Hüttenbrenner was *"almost inclined to think he had complete aversion for them."*

It is also significant that in spite of intense research and interaction with his close friends and associates, no intimate letter from the composer to a woman has surfaced, not even to those who attended the famous *"Schubertiads"* at which he sometimes played waltzes for the dancers. Apart from several letters written to his sister and stepmother, Schubert's only letters to women are quite formal ones to the German poet and playwright Helmina von Chezy and to the Austrian pianist Marie Pachler. On the contrary, there exist many tender and loving letters to his male friends -- all using rather intimate forms of address --- but not a single such letter to any woman.

It is also noteworthy that of the very few women who wrote to Schubert, none of their letters touched on sensitive or personal matters. It was perhaps because of such reasons Heinrich Kreissele, the first biographer of the composer, remarked that Schubert *"was somewhat indifferent to the charms of the fair sex"*.

All the strands of evidence on record are, therefore, so overwhelmingly one-sided in favor of a possible homosexual nature that one would wonder as to how the early biographers of Schubert chose to pay no attention to such a potentially crucial facet of his creative life. And, incredible though it may seem, it had to wait for over 160 years since his demise for some sensational facts about his private life to come out to public notice.

Franz Schubert and the Peacocks of Benvenuto Cellini

In his oft-quoted 1989 article *"Franz Schubert and the Peacocks of Benvenuto Cellini"*,[104] published in '19th Century Music', Maynard Solomon, the famous American musicologist, biographer and a co-founder of the renowned American record label 'Vanguard Records', claims Schubert was erotically attracted to men. *"The composer"*, he states, *"lived sequestered in a bohemian and homosexual circle of male friends so that he could avoid the insipid realities of life in favor of abandoned beauty and pleasure"*. Solomon writes that *"the young men of the Schubert circle loved each other"* and that *"it is reasonably probable that their primary sexual orientation was a homosexual one,"* with the young composer *"in the grip of a hunger for youth and an insatiable sexual appetite."*

---

[104] Solomon, M.: "*Franz Schubert and the peacocks of Benvenuto Cellini*", 19th Century Music 12, 1989, p. 193–206.

Maynard Solomon

In his article, Solomon further contends that for fear of exposure, members of Schubert's circle used to communicate in a code. For example, Schubert's friend Eduard von Bauernfeld remarked in his diary in August, 1826: *"Schubert is out of sorts—he needs 'young peacocks,' like Benvenuto Cellini."* The sixteenth-century sculptor Benvenuto Cellini was admittedly a homosexual, and in his autobiography of 1562, he talked of hunting 'peacocks' --- which Solomon interprets as searching for homosexual partners, especially boys dressed as women.

Solomon's article reflecting the deviant sexual orientation of the composer is important as it helps us to understand why Schubert confined himself within his own group, why he failed to meet Beethoven – though they lived in the same city for nearly thirty years ---why Beethoven's nephew wrote in a conversation book for 1823: *"They greatly praise Schubert, but it is said that he conceals himself."*

There is no doubt Schubert and his friends lived in *"a clandestine realm, one constantly beset by a variety of fears – of surveillance, of arrest and persecution, of stigmatization and exile."* It now seems that these were not really idle concerns for in early 19th Century Vienna -- dominated by the religious dictates of the church -- the sexual deviation of Schubert and his companions could well have spelled considerable trouble for them.

Schubert's nature had for too long remained hazy, shadowy and unfocused. It is also well-nigh impossible to trace Schubert's character within his music. But, in the light of the revelations brought to the fore by Solomon in his article, it is now transparent that Schubert's compulsive hedonism was a part of his nature and arguably, *"his hedonism closely paralleled the obsessiveness of his prodigious creativity"*. In the words of Solomon: *"... if gluttony was central to Schubert's personality, it was gluttony not only for food and drink, for pleasure and rapture, but for beauty and music as well."*

Schubert's 'reckless physicality', according to Solomon, may in a way be viewed *"as a compensation for his labors and deprivations, as his way of [...] needing to emerge from the secluded space of his own creativity."* His pleasure-seeking drive for *'peacocks'* may well represent *"his drive towards physical extinction, his way of hastening death even while seeking to delay it."* And it may well be *"the ultimate sign of the exercise of Schubert's free will --- his decision to live and die in his own way, unrestrainedly, proudly and creatively."*

Schubert's homosexuality: A Rebuttal

The theory put forward by Solomon that Schubert was homosexual has been hotly debated.

Noted Schubert scholar Rita Steblin challenges Solomon's proposition contending that Cellini hunted game for its medicinal value. In German folk Medicine, eating peacock flesh was thought to cure illness, and this was what, Steblin claims, an ailing Schubert also needed. In her article "The Peacock's Tale: Schubert's Sexuality Reconsidered" published in '19th Century Music' in 1993, she draws attention to the fact that in his youth Schubert had contemplated marriage to the singer Therese Grob, but couldn't because of a new law of 1815 that required an aspiring bridegroom to show he had a minimum amount of steady finances to support a family.[105]

Steblin further points out that the same Eduard Bauernfeld's diary which was relied upon by Solomon to develop his theory regarding Schubert's homosexuality also contains entries from February 1828 that unequivocally reveal that the composer was seriously in love with his pupil Caroline Esterházy and he dedicated his 'Fantasie' in F minor, written in early 1828, to Caroline. Based on this, Steblin strongly refutes Solomon's theory and asserts that Schubert was no gay -- and that he was in fact "*chasing women*". She contends further that, apart from his other escapades, Schubert also had a relationship "*on the side*" with working-class girls – a chambermaid in the Esterhazy summer palace, named '*Josepha Pepi Pöckelhofer*' in particular. Like Caroline, Pepi also received several pieces of music from Schubert that were dedicated to her. Pepi also ended up marrying someone else, as Schubert's love for her was unrequited.[106]

Rita Steblin

As against Steblin's challenge to Solomon's hypothesis that Schubert was a gay, Robert Winter's article titled "*Whose Schubert?*" is

---

[105] Steblin, Rita: "*The Peacock's Tale: Schubert's Sexuality Reconsidered*", 19th Century Music, Berkeley, California: University of California Press, 1993, p. 5-33

[106] Steblin, Rita, "*Schubert's Pepi: His Love Affair with the Chambermaid Josepha Pöckelhofer and Her Surprising Fate*". The Musical Times, 2008, p. 47–69.

essentially a reinforcement of what Solomon's article promotes.[107] Winter points out several flaws in Steblin's paper, questions her logic and is of the view that the tone of Steblin's article: *"resonates with the desire to protect the other-worldly resting place in which we have embalmed the composer. Her world is a black-and-white fantasy land that admits of no ambiguity, no irony, no double entendre. Because the only kind of evidence apparently acceptable to her – explicit references by Schubert or those in his immediate circle to same-sex eroticism--.is precisely what Schubert's world would not have allowed, she runs no risk of having to address seriously any of Solomon's evidence. Armed with this implacable preconception, she can conclude that "to put it bluntly, there is no evidence that Schubert or the members of his circle were homosexual"*.

The issue is still debated, but the hypothesis of Schubert's homosexuality has now begun to influence the interpretation of his work in scholarly papers. And, taking a cue from Solomon's work, a number of scholars on Schubert at present believe that the composer may have contracted his syphilis from a male prostitute.

Schubert's sexuality: New evidence

Interestingly, in course of the present study on Schubert, I chanced upon a note titled *"The death of Schubert"*, published in the *"Journal of the Royal Society of Medicine"* in 1990, by the famous epidemiologist R. Schoental of Royal Veterinary College, Toxicology Research Unit, Medical Research Council Laboratories, Surrey, England, in which the clinical symptoms of the ailing Schubert, shortly before his death (as recorded in Marek's biography of the composer), have been analyzed.[108] According to Professor Schoental, the symptoms are, overwhelmingly suggestive of Schubert's probable indulgence in homosexual pursuits --- with the

---

[107] Winter, Robert S.: *"Whose Schubert?"* 19th-Century Music, Vol. 17 No. 1, Summer, 1993; Published by University of California Press, p. 94-101.

[108] Schoental, R.: *"The death of Schubert"*, Journal of the Royal Society of Medicine, Vol. 83, December, 1990, p.813.

needle of suspicion pointed at his close friend Franz von Schober. To my mind, this is a fascinating new perspective for further research on Schubert's sexuality, hitherto not reflected in any of the biographies or other writings on the composer published so far.

Schoental's hypothesis is in consonance with Josef Kenner's account of Schubert's relationship with Schober. In May 1858, in response to the Austrian biographer Ferdinand Luib's request for his recollections of Schubert and his circle, Kenner wrote two long letters in which he launched violent attacks on Schober and was highly critical of his influence on Schubert. In these two letters, in no uncertain terms, he blamed Schober for encouraging young Schubert into the pathways that led to his final illness. Significantly, from the clinical standpoint too, Professor Schoental came to the same conclusion that the intriguing relationship between Schober and the young Schubert was probably the root cause of the hapless composer's premature death. This is an entirely new dimension not studied by any of the biographers of Schubert so far, and we shall visit it in greater detail in a subsequent section as we would discuss the possible causes of Schubert's death.[109][110]

Though nearly two hundred years have passed since his demise, the evidence regarding the exact nature of Schubert's sex life, as on date, is scant and, therefore, no definite conclusion can be reached. But one can be reasonably sure that there was a chasm between his public and private life. There was definitely a hedonistic side to Schubert. His contemporary German journalist, poet and playwright Helmina von Chézy, wrote that the composer *"honoured women and wine"*. On the other hand, a lot of scholars today are inclined to believe he indulged in homosexual pursuits. Perhaps he was bisexual—perhaps he was just a confused and curious artist, like many of them are, and '*tried both dishes from life's buffet*'.

---

[109] Maerk, George: "*Schubert*", 1 Nov 199, published by Viking Adult, 1 November 1991.

[110] Clive, Peter: "*Schubert and His World: A Biographical Dictionary*", Clarendon Press, Oxford, 1997, p. 93.

To ascertain the truth, there is a need for further research. But one thing must be admitted. As Winter in his article *"Whose Schubert?"* has rightly observed:

> "*Solomon has put the issue of Schubert's sexuality squarely into play, and we are all in his debt for having pondered what others merely glossed over. Although some may continue to try and put the genie back in the bottle, such efforts are certain to fail. We need to learn a great deal more about the prevailing attitudes toward gender and sexuality in Schubert's Vienna. .. [The] debate is not about "whose Schubert," [but] about replacing the stereotype of the carefree, certifiably heterosexual figure ...with the stereotype figure of the gay low-life --- with which some try to imprison Solomon --- but about liberating Schubert from all stereotypes that shield us from his enduring art.*"[111][112]

---

[111] Steblin, Rita: "*Schubert's Problematic Relationship with Johann Mayrhofer: New Documentary Evidence*". Barbara Haggh (ed.): Essays on Music and Culture in Honor of Herbert Kellman. Paris-Tours: Minerve, p. 465–495.

[112] Horton, Julian (2015): *"Schubert"*, Routledge, p. 66.

Chapter 14
Schubert's faith

Schubert disdained many aspects of traditional bourgeois life, particularly regular employment, institutional religion, conformist thinking, and perhaps marriage too. Freedom—political, personal, professional, and creative—was extremely important to the way he sought to live his life. Because of his non-conformist thinking and scorn for institutional religion, Schubert's religious belief has often been a suspect.

Was Schubert religious? It has been questioned. The answer is not easy. As with other areas of his personal life, direct evidence concerning Schubert's religious beliefs is hard to come by. At times he found it difficult to accept what he saw as the harsh and dogmatic aspects of the Catholic Church, often challenging the established views of the church.

Graham Johnson states that Schubert *"had moments of real anger and bitterness associated with religion and its hypocrisies and false promises."* About two centuries later, many people today would agree with Schubert's religious attitudes and criticisms. Peter Paul Kasper even made the bold statement that *"people learned theology from the musical prodigy, Franz Schubert."*[113][114][115]

---

[113] Johnson, Graham: *"Program notes to Schubert, Hagars Klage"*, Performed by Christine Brewer, soprano, Graham Johnson, piano. The Hyperion Schubert Edition, 31. London: Hyperion Records, CDJ33031, 1998.

[114] Moon, Jason Jye-Sung: *"A Guide to Franz Schubert's Religious Songs"*, Unpublished Dissertation submitted to the faculty of the Indiana University Jacobs School of Music in partial fulfillment of the requirements for the degree 'Doctor of Music' in Voice, December 2013, p.13.

[115] Kasper, Peter Paul. *"Schubert und die Religion."* Singende Kirche 44, no. 3 (1997): 167–168

Schubert's Church Music

Schubert's father was a devout Catholic, and the young genius grew up singing in the choir of the imperial court chapel in Vienna. He attended mass regularly as a child and continued the practice even during his adulthood, especially while living with or visiting his family. He was also occupied with the composition of music for the church from his 15th year onward until the end of his life. By the time he was 19, he had already composed four complete settings of the Catholic Mass text. He composed two more before he died. In volume, his liturgical output falls only slightly short of Mozart and greatly exceeds that of Beethoven.

It is really amazing that within his short life span, Schubert wrote so many Masses and composed such a large amount of other Catholic music; yet like Beethoven and Mozart, he was a sceptic. In his *'Dictionary of Music and Musicians'*, Sir George Grove says that "*of formal or dogmatic religion we can find no trace*" in Schubert's life. He quotes Schubert saying of creeds and churches, "*Not a word of it is true.*"

On the other hand, the noted German author Elly Ziese points out in 'Shubert's Tod' (death) that Catholic biographers of Schubert are generally of the view that the man who wrote the beautiful '*Ave Maria*' must have been a Catholic --- although "*he has no external connection with the Church.*" It is, however, not quite convincing for by the same logic one might as well say that all the artists who painted beautiful Venuses must have believed in the goddess Venus.

Some critics point to the fact that Schubert deliberately left out a key phrase, namely, "*Et in unam sanctam catholicam et apostolicamecclesiam*" ("in one holy catholic and apostolic church"), from the '*Credo*' in all of his masses, and there are other significant omissions elsewhere including the reference to the resurrection of the dead in both the E flat Mass and its predecessor in A flat. Moreover, he once wrote ""*Man resembles a ball, to be played with by fate and chance.*" They are, therefore, sceptic about Schubert's religious beliefs.

There are, however, several others who are of the opinion Schubert was a deeply religious man. They point out that in an 1815 diary entry, Schubert wrote:

> *"It is with faith that man first enters the world. It comes long before reason and knowledge, for to understand something one must first believe something ... reason is nothing other than analyzed faith."*

An ardent admirer of Schubert's religious music, the great Austrian conductor Nikolaus Harnoncourt strongly believed that down deep, Schubert was a devout man: *"you can hear it in the Mass No. 5 in A-flat"*.

According to Harnoncourt, the Mass No. 5, D 678 provides a deeply moving experience right from the start because of how Schubert sets the opening expression --- *'kyrie eleison, christe, eleison'* ('Oh Lord, have mercy'). In his words:[116]

> *"I think this mass is the witness of fighting for more belief and more religious feeling. Religion is not a gift you get ready-made; it is a question of searching. And I think Schubert was a deeply religious man."*

---

[116] Huizenga, Tom: "*Nikolaus Harnoncourt: Schubert's Religion*", published in 'The NPR Music Newsletter', May 11, 2006.

Nikolaus Harnoncourt

The exact position, however, one must admit, is still not very clear. Scholars and fans of Franz Schubert's music, therefore, continue to debate the nature of his religious beliefs.

And the debate continues to this day.[117][118][119]

---

[117] Gibbs, Christopher H.: *"The Life of Schubert"*, Cambridge University Press, March 2015.

[118] Grove, George: *"Grove's Dictionary of Music and Musicians"*, Published by Franklin Classics Trade Press, 31 October, 2018.

[119] Ziese, Elly: *"Schubert's death and burial in the oldest depiction"*, published by Gotland Vlg., Großdeuben, circa 1933.

Chapter 15
Death of Franz Schubert

By 1828, Schubert's creative spree had reached its pinnacle. About this time his health also deteriorated. He developed constant headaches, intermittent fever and indisposition. In the late summer of 1828, he saw the court physician Ernst Rinna, who apparently confirmed his suspicion that he was ill beyond cure and was likely to die soon.

In November, his symptoms multiplied -- he experienced headache, fever, swollen joints, and vomiting. With each passing day, his condition worsened. Unable to retain solid food, he had to practically starve towards the end, and ultimately died at the age of 31 at the apartment of his brother Ferdinand. By his own request, he was buried next to Beethoven, whom he adored all his life.

Schubert's life was as such haunted by varying periods of sickness. In 1822 he began to suffer from headaches, intermittent fever and skin rash. The next year, his scalp began to itch so intensely that he had his patchy head shaved and bought a wig. He was subsequently admitted to Vienna General Hospital where he wrote part of *'Die schöne Müllerin'* ('The Beautiful Maid of the Mill'). So he had to battle with illness practically throughout the last several years of his life.

Despite his continuing ill-health, Schubert did not give in and continued with his creativity composing sensational musical pieces one after another – some of the best the world of music will ever experience. It was in the genre of the *'lied'* that Schubert made his most indelible mark. American musicologist Leon Plantinga is of the view that "*in his more than six hundred Lieder he [Schubert] explored and expanded the potentialities of the genre, as no composer before him.*"

But being a victim of repeated incidents of misfortune, rejections and lack of recognition throughout his life, Schubert was emotionally shattered and was fast losing hope. As mentioned earlier, he became a patient of *cyclothymia,* a mental illness that resulted in severe mood swings fluctuating between hypomania and depression.

Schubert's condition became far more extreme during his mid-twenties, and his friends reported periods of dark despair and violent anger. His continuing illness only exacerbated the problem. Physically, Schubert's life was haunted by varying periods of sickness. In 1822, he began to suffer from headaches, intermittent fever and skin rash. The next year, his scalp began to itch so intensely, that he had his patchy head shaved and bought a wig. As his problem still persisted, he was subsequently admitted to Vienna General Hospital, where he wrote part of '*Die schöne Müllerin*'. Thus he had to battle with the illness throughout his life.[120]

Towards the end, Schubert had given up hope of recovery and wrote to a friend:

> *"I am the most unhappy and miserable person in this world... my health will never improve, and in such despair, things will only become worse instead of better..."*

On 19 November 1828, Schubert died in Vienna at the apartment of his brother Ferdinand. He was only 31 when he died.

---

[120] Ho, Desiree: "*Franz Schubert's Illness: The Melancholy of an Autumnal Sunset*", Published in 'Interlude', 7 October 2011.

Chapter 16
The Mystery surrounding Schubert's death

There is still a mystery about the exact cause of Schubert's death. Officially, the cause of his death was typhoid, though other theories have also been proposed, including the tertiary stage of syphilis -- and, interestingly, certain documents accessed by us in course of the present study on Schubert suggest that he might even have been a victim of AIDS.

Typhoid?

Though his health was failing and he was suffering from headaches, intermittent fever, indigestion and other ailments, still there is a kind of suddenness in Schubert's death. On 31October 1828, while dining at a tavern, he became ill - the fish he had just begun eating filled him with a sensation as though he had taken poison. But it seems he recovered soon. On 3 November he attended a concert and the following day the ever curious Schubert attended a music lesson as he wanted to study again - for he thought he didn't know enough about fugue and counterpoint.

On 9 November he had dinner at Baron Schönstein's home. Though he could not eat much, he looked fine and cheerful. But on November 11, suffering from nausea and headache, he took to his bed in the house of his brother Ferdinand. Five days later the doctor who treated Schubert diagnosed '*nervenfieber*' as the cause of his death -- that's how typhoid fever was called at that time. There wasn't any epidemic in Vienna at that time but isolated cases were frequent. It was not unusual for typhoid to be spread by drinking contaminated water and water then wasn't always safe enough. In fact, Schubert's mother and his brother Ferdinand both had also died of *'nervenfieber'*.[121]

So, according to the earliest version, Schubert died of typhoid. Indeed, the symptoms of Schubert's illness matched those of typhoid and one more fact reinforces this theory -- his hypochondriac friend Schober didn't visit him, afraid of being infected.

Syphilis?

There are, however, several arguments against the diagnosis of 'typhoid' as the cause of Schubert's death. Most significantly, *'nervenfieber'* (*'nerve fever'*) as diagnosed by his treating physician was at that time in use as a very non-specific term referring to a concurrence of fever and cerebral symptoms. Some biographers and scholars are of the view that Schubert's *'nervenfieber'* was perhaps a symptom of *'meningovascular syphilis'* -- 'a chronic form of syphilis infection that affects the central nervous system' -- occurring on an average seven years after the primary syphilis infection. This, in their opinion, also explains Schubert's prodromal symptoms of headaches, vertigo and intermittent focal symptoms, 'aphonia' ('inability to speak due to damage to the larynx or mouth') and his inability to play the piano for a while, as well as the final therapeutics given to him including ointments and vesicant plasters.[122]

Based on the preponderance of such evidence, it came to be widely believed Schubert died of syphilis. Several scholars are of the view that the early impression that he died of typhoid was perhaps based partly on ignorance, and partly to protect the composer's dignity and honour. Although syphilis was prevalent in Vienna at that time, the disease was so stigmatizing that after his death, Schubert's friends burnt his letters

---

[121] Bogousslavsky, Julien, Hennerici, M. G., Baezner, H., Bassetti, C. (Ed.): "*Neurological Disorders in Famous Artists*", Part 3, Karger, 2010, p. 77.

[122] Hetenyi, G.: "*The terminal illness of Franz Schubert and the treatment of syphilis in Vienna in the eighteen hundred and twenties*".
https://www.utpjournals.press/doi/pdf/10.3138/cbmh.3.1.51

and diaries so that the true nature of his illness could never be officially identified.

Before we delve into the issue further, it ought to be noted that it is by now fairly well established that Schubert had contracted syphilis from a prostitute, most probably in late 1822 or early 1823.[123] In the 1820s there were over ten thousand prostitutes in Vienna. But to the contemporary Viennese society of Schubert's time, syphilis was highly stigmatized. One may, therefore, imagine the profound sense of shame that must have pervaded his life when he contracted syphilis. When the symptoms of syphilis first appeared, Schubert stayed at home and hid from his friends. Patchy hair loss prompted him to buy a wig. In the spring of 1823, he even had to be admitted to Vienna General Hospital for treatment. There is, therefore, no controversy over the fact that Schubert was syphilitic. The debate is only over the question if the terminal cause of his death was syphilis -- or was it due to any other reason, like typhoid, etc.

Schubert was an introvert and not very attractive. Standing at barely five feet tall, he was a shy, stumpy person whose facial features included "*a round nose, a long oval face and a deeply cleft chin*". Romance was difficult for him, and perhaps that was why he turned to prostitutes and eventually contracted the sexually transmitted disease 'syphilis'.

This apart there is another important point to be considered. The doctor who visited Schubert during the last week before his death was not the regular doctor Reena, as he was sick. Instead of him, a new doctor who was also a specialist in venereal disease came to see Schubert towards the end. Was it by chance, or was it that the composer's brother Ferdinand summoned him because of his expertise? But then a pertinent question is, if he was an expert in syphilis, why then he would certify vague '*nervenfieber*' as the cause of his death instead of syphilis

---

[123] Sams, Eric: "*Schubert's Illness Re-Examined*", The Musical Times, Vol. 121, No. 1643, January 1980.

unless it really was *'nervenfieber- typhoid fever'?* These are questions for which there seems to be no straightforward answer.

Those opposed to the theory that Schubert died of syphilis point out, in the first stage of syphilis, 'chancres' -- a painless ulcer, particularly one that develops on the genitals in venereal disease-- develop within a few weeks after infection. Secondary syphilis has some symptoms very similar to those of flu and also causes skin lesions and hair loss. After that, the symptoms disappear and it seems that the patient is cured. This latent phase may last from a few months to decades until tertiary syphilis arrives. Sometimes this last phase is relatively benign, but it usually affects the nervous system or the heart, and death comes in a few years.

But Schubert was apparently not in any of these situations. Moreover, tertiary syphilis manifests, on average, fifteen years after primary syphilis, while Schubert had been infected with syphilis only five years before. So the available evidence does not conclusively support the theory that Schubert died of syphilis.

Sounds intriguing? Well, it is still not over. There is yet another theory in vogue --- Schubert died of "mercury poisoning".

Mercury poisoning?

In today's world, syphilis is no longer the menace it used to be because an early prescription of penicillin is sufficient to treat the condition. But the most common treatment available in the days gone by was quite horrific. The patient would be confined in a sealed room, and his body would be covered with mercury. The patient was forbidden to even change his undergarment or bed sheets.

The mercury treatment often caused the patient's mouth cavity to heat up and the taste of metal would adversely affect his appetite. The side effects included mouth cavity pains, difficulty in swallowing, excessive drooling, diarrhea, vomiting, and excess urination. The doctors would explain to the patients that these were simply side consequences of effective treatment. But, in fact, these were symptoms of 'mercury poisoning'.

Schubert lived his final days in a tightly sealed room. He had lost his appetite for more than ten days. During the last few weeks of his life, he often puked up most of the food that he ate. About two weeks before he died, he tried to eat supper, but with a look of disgust placed his knife and fork on the plate and did not accept food or drink ever again. On his final day, he screamed intermittently and then died.

After his death, many articles claim that Schubert died of *'typhus abdominalis'*[124], but such a disease was not prevalent in Vienna then, nor did he possess the symptoms typical of *typhus abdominalis*.

Therefore, though Schubert had contracted syphilis, many scholars are of the opinion it was probably the mistreatment of his disease leading to mercury poisoning that really caused his death.[125]

According to Dr. Gabe Mirkin, MD, the well-known American sports medicine doctor and fitness guru, Schubert exhibited many symptoms very similar to mercury poisoning. In his considered view, therefore, *"most likely Schubert died of mercury poisoning that can damage the brain, heart, kidneys, lungs, and immune system in the same way that syphilis does."*

AIDS?

Before we conclude our discussion on the probable causes of Schubert's death, I would like to draw your attention to an interesting article (supra) that I chanced to come across in course of the present inquiry into the *"Life, Death and the Last words of Franz Schubert"*.

---

[124] 'Typhus' is a disease caused by infection with one or more rickettsial bacteria. Fleas, mites (chiggers), lice, or ticks transmit it when they bite a person. Typhus is not infectious like cold or the flu. The common symptoms of Typhus include severe headache, fever, swollen lymph nodes, chills, cough, rash, diarrhea, weariness, confusion, etc.

[125] Mirkin, Dr. Gabe: *"Franz Schubert, Syphilis and Mercury Poisoning"*. https://shorturl.at/ajEK4

The article sheds new light on the probable cause of the young composer's untimely death. Written by the renowned epidemiologist R. Schoental of Royal Veterinary College, Toxicology Research Unit, Medical Research Council Laboratories, Surrey, this article titled "*The death of Schubert*" was published in the prestigious "*Journal of the Royal Society of Medicine*" in 1990, and it adds an amazingly new dimension to the mystery surrounding Schubert's death, not reflected in any of the biographies of the composer published till date.[126]

In an insightful analysis of the clinical symptoms as well as the events leading to the composer's death, Professor Schoental points out in his article that Schubert's biographer, Marek, mentioned in his book that the young genius spent most of his time in Vienna in a circle of aristocratic '*bon vivants*', some of whom had homosexual leanings. In his note, Schoental particularly raises his finger of suspicion towards Schubert's closest friend, Franz von Schober, a charming dilettante of about the same age as the young composer, who befriended Schubert and extended to him the hospitality in his home (rather his mother's home).

Schoental draws our attention further to the subsequent events as described in Maerk's biography of the young composer to show that as Schubert stayed with Schober from 1821 to 1823, he became seriously ill. Syphilis was suspected for which he was treated. Though he improved and continued for some time with his creative pursuits, but a subsequent spell of Schober's hospitality resulted in deterioration of his heath. Towards the end, in September 1828 he went to live with his brother Ferdinand, but developed abdominal pain, intractable diarrhea etc., within a few weeks, and finally he died on 19 November 1828 when he was only 31. His friend Schober remained unmarried till he was about 58 years of age, and lived to the advanced age of 86 years.

---

[126] Schoental, R.: "*The death of Schubert*", Journal of the Royal Society of Medicine, Vol. 83, December 1990, p.813.

Continuing further, Schoental states the rapid course of Schubert's stomach disorder as apparent from Marek's biography is suggestive of his low immune status. This, he suspects, may well be due to the young genius being a victim of 'AIDS'. In his article in the "*Journal of the Royal Society of Medicine*" (supra), Schoental writes:

> "*The recent outbreak of AIDS among the modern gay communities focused attention on the importance of the immune system and its vulnerability to a variety of toxic factors, whether exogenous or formed endogenously, under specific conditions. It is usually the passive partners (the 'catamites') who are the main sufferers of AIDS. The poor, 'defenceless' Schubert, preoccupied with his musical creation, might possibly have died of AIDS. How to prove, or disprove this hypothesis*"?

From the accounts of Schubert's intimate friends and acquaintances as well as from the writings of the biographers and researchers on Schubert, it is by now fairly well established that Schubert had a secret life that kept him outside the bounds of bourgeois society. For much of his career, he was intimately associated with a circle of artists in which homosexuality was, if not the norm, at any rate not an exception. His dearest friend, Schober with whom he lived for several long periods until shortly before his death in 1828, was homosexual. A brilliant talker and an affluent patron, Schober had an abiding influence on the young composer and might well have led him into depravity. Schoental's proposition that Schubert died of AIDS, therefore, seems to have much substance.

Franz von Schober   Franz Peter Schubert

Schubert is dead and gone. The cause of his death is no more than of academic interest today. It is, however, a pity that during his life-time the contemporary world of music failed to recognize his genius though it is now widely acknowledged that his premature death caused irreparable harm to the music world. Throughout his life Schubert lived in penury. Publishers were reluctant to print his works for he was not so well known at that time. He, therefore, had no choice but to turn to his friends to print his works. We are not too sure if because of his financial distress, the immature Schubert was compelled to succumb to the carnal desire and sexual exploitation by his wealthy friends as Schoental's research seems to suggest. It would surely be most unfortunate if that was the case with the young genius.

Be that as it may, Schubert, as a true genius with a rare indomitable spirit, never allowed his misfortune to take its toll on his creativity. So, during the last months of his life, even in his worst hours, he composed such heavenly music as the great quintet in G-major and the strangely haunting tragic melodies of *"Die Winterreise"* ('The winter journey'). And incredible though it may seem, a week before his death, he revised a brief work for a choir and was correcting the proofs of the second set of his song cycle '*Die Winterreise*' -- but shortly thereafter he became delirious and died.[127][128]

American Music critic Philip Hale in a brilliant piece on Schubert's work beautifully captures the last moments of the composer's life:

> "*...Schubert smelled the mould and knew the earth was impatiently looking for him...it is the melancholy of an autumnal sunset, of the ironical depression due to a burgeoning noon in the spring, the melancholy that comes between the lips of lovers.*"

----

[127] Maerk, George R.: "*Schubert*", published by Viking Adult, 1 November 1991.
[128] Greenberg, Robert: "*Music History Monday: Schubert's Death*", Published in 'Medium Music' 19 November 2018.

Chapter 17
The Last wish of Franz Schubert

"No, no. It is not true. This is not Beethoven lying here!"

On October 19, 1828, Schubert passed away in Vienna --- at the age of only 31.

Sometime in the late summer of 1822, the 25-year-old young composer contracted syphilis during a nocturnal pleasure jaunt with his friend Franz von Schober. The primary symptoms of Schubert's syphilis appeared in December of 1822. In 1823 he had to be admitted in hospital for treatment. But then — from the fall of 1824 until mid-1827 or so — the disease entered its dormant phase and consequently, for about three years, Schubert was noninfectious and there was no manifestation of the disease.

Though his general well-being had improved, Schubert still suffered from depression, exacerbated by the fear that the disease would visit him again. To avoid pain, he used to self-medicate -- with nicotine and by drinking far too much alcohol that made the otherwise ordinarily mild-mannered Schubert vulgar, abusive, and destructive. An intoxicated young Schubert, it is said, would often indulge in smashing glassware and crockery, for which he became — and understandably so — a less-than-welcome guest in Vienna's homes, pubs, and restaurants.

Nevertheless, for nearly three years during the dormancy of his disease, Schubert was able to lead a normal life. In March of 1825 Johanna Lutz, his friend and a *"Schubertian"* (a member of the 'Friends of Franz Schubert' group) -- wrote to her fiancé the famous Austrian painter Leopold Kupelwieser who was also a close friend of the composer: *"Schubert is now very busy and well-behaved, which pleases me very much."*

A few months later Schubert's friend Anton von Ottenwalt, who was also the poet of the Schubert song, *"Der Knabe in der Wiege"* ('The boy in the cradle') composed in 1817, gleefully wrote in a letter to a friend:

> *"Schubert looks so well and strong, is so nice and cheerful and so genially communicative that one cannot fail to be delighted."*

The dormancy of his disease perhaps gave the composer hope -- hope that he would be among those lucky few for whom the dreadful disease once dormant did not recur. But, alas, it was not to be.

During the summer of 1827, Schubert began experiencing repeated headaches. By the end of July, it was clear that his syphilis was once again advancing. Despite his illness, in August and September of 1828, Schubert accomplished what would seem to be a miraculous feat. Within a period of only about six weeks, he composed his last three piano sonatas — in C Minor, A Major, and B-flat Major, D. 958, 959 and 960, six songs from the collection *"Schwanengesang" ('Swan Song')*, *D.957* and his final chamber work, the majestic String Quintet in C Major, *D. 956*, Op. posth. 163 -- sometimes called the "Cello Quintet".

Despite his failing health, Schubert continued to remain cheerful. In early October 1828, he even joined some friends for a three-day walking tour of Lower Austria to visit Joseph Haydn's grave in Eisenstadt. But on October 31, while dining at a tavern *"Zum roten Kreuz"* ('The Red Cross'), he suddenly threw his knife and fork down onto the plate, and said the fish he had just begun eating filled him with such disgust and horror, as though he had taken poison. Later, after his death, Schubert's brother Ferdinand stated that Franz's terminal illness began at that moment.

On 3 November he set off early in the morning and walked from Neu-Wieden where he was staying at that time, to the Parish Church in Hernals, a three-hour walk, to listen to a performance of a Latin requiem, composed by his brother Ferdinand --- the last music that he ever heard.

On November 5, Schubert took to his bed with a fever. Little did he know that his tertiary syphilis and the toxic, mercury-based treatment he was undergoing for syphilis had completely ravaged his immune system leading to fatal consequences.

On November 11, Schubert's friend Josef von Spaun came to visit. He found Franz correcting proofs for the second part of the song cycle *Winterreise*. Spaun later wrote:

> *"I found him ill in bed, though his condition didn't seem to me at all serious. [....] I left him without any anxiety at all, and it came as a thunderbolt when, a few days later, I heard of his death. Poor Schubert, so young and at the start of a brilliant career! What a wealth of untapped treasures his death has robbed us of!"*

Over the next few days, his condition fast deteriorated. On November 19, 1828, at three o'clock in the afternoon, Schubert died. He was only 31 then.

Schubert died on a Wednesday. On 20 November 1828, the day following his death, his father had the painful duty of issuing the obituary notice. It was mentioned in the notice the body of the deceased will be taken on the next day for burial near the bishop's stall in the parish church of St. Josef in Margareten, where the holy rites would be performed.

But it did not happen as planned. Two days later on Friday, November 21 — the day scheduled for the funeral --- Schubert's brother Ferdinand's letter describing the last moments of his beloved brother reached their father early in the morning.

Ferdinand wrote in his letter Schubert had been delirious near the end and that before he breathed his last, he wished to rest by the side of

Beethoven, whom he so greatly revered. Describing the last moments of his beloved brother, Ferdinand wrote:

> *"On the evening before his death, though only half-conscious, he said to me: "I implore you to take me to my room, not to leave me here, in this corner under the earth. Do I, then, deserve no place above the earth?" I answered him: "Dear Franz, rest assured, believe me, believe your brother Ferdinand, whom you have always trusted and who loves you so much, you are in the room which you have always been in so far and lie in your bed!"*

But Schubert was not convinced. He wanted to go out. It seemed he was under the illusion he was in a strange room -- and was being buried alive. He felt himself close to Beethoven's grave. Beethoven – whom he adored throughout his life.

The doctor tried to reassure him and said he would recover if he stayed quietly in bed. But Schubert, in a state of delirium-- cried out: "*Here, here is my end.*" Later, he asked to be placed in his own bed. When assured that he already was there, in his delirious state, he exclaimed:

> "*No, no. It is not true. This is not Beethoven lying here!*"

These were his last words.

> *"Could this be anything but an indication of his inmost wish to rest by the side of Beethoven, whom he so greatly revered?"*
> Ferdinand asked in his letter.

Schubert's 'dying wish' was granted. The funeral took place on the day appointed, but the place of burial was changed. In deference to his last wish, Schubert was buried in the '*Währing* Cemetery'-- just three graves away from Beethoven.

Chapter 18
Funeral

It was a day of unusually bad weather. The gloomy dark sky was pouring heavily as if the entire world was in a state of mourning to pay homage to the departed soul.

And after what must have been a hasty arrangement following a last-minute change of site, there at Wahring, in bad weather, Schubert's remains were laid to rest, in deference to his last wishes, close beside Beethoven's grave -- only three places distant from it.

The funeral took place on Friday, November 21. A crowd of relations, friends and sympathizers had assembled to take a last view of the body, which lay *"dressed in the clothing of a hermit, with a laurel-wreath round his head, as if asleep, with the face still unchanged by death, more like a sleeping than a dead man"*.

The coffin, covered with many garlands, left the house at half-past two. It was borne by his friends, pupils, and associates, mostly young men, in red cloaks and flowers, to the local parish church of St. Josef zu Margareten, where the funeral service was performed.

'St. Joseph Margaret parish church'

Inside there is a plaque commemorating the consecration of Franz Schubert

A church organ Schubert used to play is also on display

Schober was chief mourner, and a hymn by him, "*Der Friede sey mit dir, du engelreine Seele*" ('Peace be with you, you pure soul') — written that morning in substitution for his own earlier words -- was sung to the music of Schubert's own song "*Pax Vobiscum*," ('Peace be with you') with an accompaniment of wind instruments, before the interment. Gansbacher, Domkapellmeister ("Master of Choristers") of the local church, conducted the funeral music. The friends, relatives, and admirers who had assembled then offered a prayer and carried the body to the "*Währinger Ortsfriedhof*" -- the 'local cemetery' in the village of Wahring, where after another commendatory prayer the body was consigned to grave.

Schubert's Death mask

Late in the afternoon that day, the German writer, novelist and historical essayist Wilhelm von Chezy, son of the esteemed poetess Helmina von Chezy (authoress of 'Euryanthe' and 'Rosamunde'), who though not in Schubert's most intimate circle but was one of his acquaintances, had by chance walked down to Bogner's coffee-house, where the young composer was usually to be found between 5 and 7 in the afternoon, smoking his pipe and joking with his friends. To his surprise, he found the coffee house almost deserted. On entering he was asked by the waiter—*"Sir seems to be back too soon from the funeral!"* *"Whose funeral?"* asked Chezy in astonishment. *'Franz Schubert's,'* replied the waiter, *'he died two days ago, and is buried this afternoon.'*

Schubert had left no will. The official inventory of his possessions at the time of his death, unfortunately, was too meager and comprised simply his clothes and few other small possessions worth only fifty shillings, and a bundle of unpublished manuscripts of old music including many of his great works of the last few years, valued at 8s.6d.

Imagine! A dusky bundle of unpublished manuscripts of old music by Schubert, valued at *8s. 6d.*! And for all you know this 'bundle' most probably included his timeless masterpiece like, the 'Great'-- that, on being discovered about a decade later, would churn out millions of pound sterling for its publisher in the years to come. But it was all that 'poor' Schubert had left behind to take care of his own mortal remains as well as for his family at the time of his untimely death.

More than 70 florins had been expended by Schubert's father and brother on his medical attendance and at the funeral. As the estate left by Schubert was woefully inadequate to meet the expenses, they had to approach Schubert's friends, pupils and other members of the public for financial assistance to meet the cost of his medical attendance, of the requiems performed in two churches, and the expenses for the funeral.

Chapter 19
Schubert's Epitaph

To pay tribute to the young genius, six days after the funeral, on Thursday, the 27th November, the "*Kirchen-musikverein*" ('Church Music Society'), Vienna performed Mozart's Requiem in Schubert's honour. On the 14th December, his early Symphony in C, No. 6, was played at the Gesellschafts concert, and again on March 12, 1829.

On 23 December, a Requiem for double chorus, composed by Anselm Hüttenbrenner, Director of the "Styrian Muskiverein" ('Styrian Music Society') was given by Schubert's friends and admirers at the "*Augustinerkirche*" ('St. Augustine's church') located on Josefsplatz, next to the Hofburg, the winter palace of the Habsburg dynasty in Vienna.

At Linz, a city in Upper Austria, straddling the Danube River midway between Salzburg and Vienna, on Christmas Day, there was a funeral ceremony to commemorate him with speeches and music. Articles in his honour appeared in the 'Wiener Zeitschrift' ('The Viennese Journal') of December 25, by the poet Joseph von Zedlitz, in the "Theaterzeitung" ('Theatre Newspaper') of Vienna of the 20th and 27th (by Blahetka), in the Vienna "Zeitschrift für Kunst" ('The Journal of Art') of June 9, 11, 13, 1829 by dramatist Bauernfeld, in the Vienna 'Archiv für Geschichte' ('Archive for History') by poet Mayrhofer, and memorial poems were published by poet Seidl, Schober, and others.

It was also decided to raise a monument over his grave. As Schubert's relatives did not have adequate means to defray the expenses, Frl. Anna Frohlich, a music teacher in Vienna and one of Schubert's admirers, made arrangements for a concert on January 30, 1829, in the hall of the Vienna Musikverein (Vienna Music Society), and to utilize the proceeds to meet the expenses of the proposed memorial. The programme consisted almost entirely of Schubert's music, including his 'Miriam's War song,' and several other pieces, excepting a set of Flute variations by Gabrielsky, and the first Finale in 'Don Juan'.

The concert was a grand success so much so that it had to be repeated. The proceeds of the two concerts, coupled with generous offerings from a few friends, were adequate to meet the cost of the proposed memorial.

Schubert's friend, Franz Schober, was assigned the task of selection of the particular kind of memorial to be put up. Schober, acting under the advice of the architect Heinrich von Forster, sketched a design and finished a bust that had been begun by the sculptor Arnold. The bust is the work of the sculptor Franz Dialler. Wsserburger, a master mason, finished the gravestone. The cost of the entire memorial was 360 florins 46 kr.

Franz Seraphicus Grillparzer

The bust of Schubert adorns the monument, and below it runs the following epitaph penned by the Austrian playwright and poet Grillparzer:

Original Tomb of Franz Schubert[129]

"Music has here entombed a rich treasure,

But still far fairer hopes,

Here lies Franz Schubert,

Born January 31, 1797,

Died November 19, 1828,

Aged 31 years"

Schubert's Epitaph: Criticism

"Music has here entombed a rich treasure,

But still far fairer hopes"

-- Schubert's Epitaph

---

[129] Original Tomb of Franz Schubert at former cemetery, today park Währinger Schubertpark in 18. Währing, Wien, Austria

The words on the second line of Schubert's epitaph have often met with the sharpest criticism. Reflecting on it, the great German composer, pianist, and influential music critic Robert Schumann wrote:

> *"[Schubert] was able with a calm look to confront the approach of death. And although on the slab over his grave we read of a wealthy treasure being buried with him, but hopes yet far fairer and unfulfilled, let us with gratitude only reflect on the first of these declarations."*

The epitaph was composed in 1829. Schumann wrote these words in 1838. At the time when poet Grillparzer wrote the epitaph, Schubert's rich legacy of songs had not made its way in the world of music, and, therefore, through these words in the epitaph Grillparzer had just tried to give expression to the thoughts that thousands of Schubert's friends and followers, on hearing the news of the young composer's death, had as their fondest hope.

But following posthumous publication of Schubert's major compositions, like '*Winterreise*', particularly after his priceless masterpieces, like, the '*Unfinished Symphony*', the '*Great*' etc. came to the fore, this epitaph ('the second line') by Grillparzer that seemed objectionable to Schumann many years ago, would now perhaps raise eyebrows of most other music lovers too.

Today with over 1500 published works to his credit, Schubert is reckoned as one of the greatest maestros of all time; Schumann is, therefore, justified when he says, "*To indulge in subtle speculations as to what he* [Schubert] *might have attained, is utterly valueless.*" If an artist, whose creations have won immortality for their author, he ought to be permitted to count his earthly mission fulfilled, and this undoubtedly is the case with Franz Schubert.[130][131]

Today one would, therefore, perhaps readily agree with Schumann who had rightly said, *"He [Schubert] has done enough, and praised be he who, like Schubert, has striven and accomplished."*

---

[130] Schumann, Robert von: "*Gesammelte Schriften Uber Musik Und Musiker*", ('Collected Writings on Music and Musicians'), vol. ii, Georg Wigand's Verlag. ('George Wigand Publishing House'), 1854, p. 240.

[131] Kreissle von Hellborn, Heinrich: "*The Life of Franz Schubert*", Vol. ii, Edited and Translated by Arthur D. Coleridge, Cambridge University Press, 2014, p. 150.

Chapter 20
Schubert: The 'Phoenix' that rose from the ashes

Outside of Austria, Schubert's death created at first but little sensation –except amongst some of his ardent admirers. Like Robert Schumann, then 18, is said to have *"cried all night"*, when news of Schubert's death reached him at Leipzig. "The classical Romantic" Mendelssohn too, was saddened by the untimely demise of "the Romantic classic" Schubert. And Rellstab, Anna Milder, and others in Berlin, who were fond of Schubert's music, also mourned him deeply. But the world at large did not know enough of his works at that time to realize what it had lost in that modest, self-effacing young musician of 31.

Schubert died the youngest of all the great composers — at 31. He died even younger than Mozart.

Schubert was a prolific composer; incredible though it may seem, he wrote over 1,500 works during his brief lifetime. Between 1821 and his death in 1828, more than 100 opuses of his music had been published (or at least proofed by the composer), most by Viennese firms. This was a rate unequalled by any of Schubert's Viennese contemporaries. In terms of the sheer number of opuses, it almost doubles the total for Beethoven over the same period.

Despite his prodigious output, unfortunately, the major works of Schubert remained mostly unpublished during his lifetime. In a city like Vienna where music was played nearly every night, Schubert gave just one public concert in his entire career. He never achieved success in the opera house. He never heard a professional performance of any of his symphonies. Only one of his compositions — the E-flat piano trio — was published abroad during his lifetime.

The limited popularity and success Schubert enjoyed during his brief lifetime made him one of the most neglected geniuses in the history of music. Unfortunately, therefore, in the years immediately after his death, he had more or less the image of a cardboard caricature — a poor coffee-house composer who jotted down songs, one after another, on the tablecloth or the back of a menu, while the world passed him by. Even when Joseph von Spaun reported that Schubert composed *"Der Erlkönig" "in no time at all . . . just as quickly as one can write,"* it only fanned Schubert's reputation as a facile and largely intuitive composer, as opposed to a learned, hard-working, cerebral titan like Beethoven, who sketched copiously and sweated over every note. That is why even as late as in 1894, in an influential essay, the British scholar and composer Sir Charles Hubert Hastings Parry, 1st Baronet could still maintain that Schubert had no feeling for *"abstract design, and balance and order,"* and *"no taste for the patient balancing, considering, and rewriting again and again, which was characteristic of Beethoven"* — a verdict that remained unchallenged well into the next century.

Sir Charles Hubert Hastings Parry

In this backdrop, it is no wonder that outside Austria, Schubert's death created at first but little sensation –except amongst some of his ardent admirers. But death at times increases public curiosity about an artist's works -- and so it was now. About a year or two before his death, publishers had started taking interest in Schubert, and several of them now surged forward. The stream of publication of Schubert's compositions, therefore, soon ensued, and continued to flow; and neither the supply of works nor the eagerness to obtain them have ceased till date.

As Schubert's compositions began to be published, the entire world of music – far and wide – was amazed by the mellifluous, awe-inducing music and wondered how such a treasure could remain hidden so long in those dusky heaps of music paper -- valued at 8*s*. 6*d*. -- left behind by young Schubert at the time of his death! And what a ceaseless and priceless store it was, particularly to include a masterpiece like, the '*Great*', retrieved from oblivion over a decade after the composer's death (or for that matter, the "*unfinished Symphony*" discovered several decades later). These also included other masterly compositions of Schubert ---ranging from songs, masses, operas, chamber-music to pianoforte-sonatas, duets, trios, quartets, quintet, octet, etc. –each so amazingly fresh, copious, and different from the last.[132]

But, believe it or not, it raised suspicion too.

> "*A deep shade of suspicion,*" said a leading musical periodical in 1839 "*is beginning to be cast over the authenticity of posthumous compositions. All Paris has been in a state of amazement at the posthumous diligence of the song-writer, F. Schubert, who, while one would think that his ashes repose in peace in Vienna, is still making eternal new songs.*"

Well, by now we are mostly familiar with the greatness of Schubert's genius. But imagine -- at a time when he was little known outside Austria, the doubt in the minds of the Parisians about the authenticity of his posthumous compositions was perhaps not so unnatural. It was not unnatural particularly, because the number of unpublished

---

[132] Grove, Sir George: "*Beethoven - Schubert – Mendelssohn*", Published by Read Books, 15 March 2007.

manuscripts of Schubert was so incredibly huge, and of which no one seemed to know the particulars. It was partly so because Schubert was hopelessly disorganized, and given his nature, he might, in some cases, have concealed, or even forgotten about it.

A number of Schubert's songs and pianoforte pieces were also in the hands of publishers at the time of his death. The bulk of the work left behind by him, however, was in the possession of his brother Ferdinand, as his heir. A set of 4 songs (op. 105) was issued on the day of his funeral. A number of other songs followed up to April 1829. But the first important publication was the well-known "Schwanengesang," ('Swan song') so entitled by the publisher Haslinger—a collection of 14 songs, 7 by Rellstab, 6 by Heine, and 1 by Seidl—unquestionably Schubert's last. They were published posthumously in May 1829, and, have been as much appreciated as the *'Die schöne Müllerin'* or the *'Winterreise'*. Franz Liszt later transcribed these songs for solo piano.

Another large portion of Ferdinand's possessions came, sooner or later, into the hands of Dr. Eduard Schneider, son of Franz's sister Theresia. The greater part of these manuscripts was later acquired by the Austrian industrialist and a patron of arts and music Herr Nicholas Dumba of Vienna.

Since July 10, 1830, the publisher Diabelli began to publish at intervals the unpublished manuscripts of Schubert. By 1850, he published, in 50 parts, 137 of Schubert's songs. In 1830 he had also published two astonishing 4-hand marches (op. 121), and a set of 20 waltzes (op. 127); whilst other houses published the PF. Sonatas in A and E♭ (op. 120, 122); two string quartets of the year 1824 (op. 125); the D minor Quartet, etc.

A decade after Schubert's demise, Schumann visited Vienna and met Schubert's brother Ferdinand in the late autumn of 1838. Schumann's visit marks a watershed in the history of Schubert's music. It was he who first noticed the immense heap of manuscripts which was lying with Ferdinand – and amongst them, there were several symphonies too. Schumann picked out several of these works to recommend to publishers, but there was one particular composition in the 'bundle' that riveted his attention— the 'Symphony No. 9 in C major', D 944, the *'Great'*, the final symphony completed by *Schubert* in March 1828.

Schumann persuaded Ferdinand to give him a copy of the symphony, the 'Great', and took it to Leipzig, where the entire work was performed publicly for the first time by Mendelssohn, at the concert hall in Leipzig on 21 March 1839, more than a decade after Schubert's death, and repeated three times during the following season.

Schumann had long been an ardent admirer of Schubert. His journal *"Die Nieu Zeitschrift fur Musik"* ("New Journal for Music") often contained articles on Schubert's music; when 'Great was performed it was highly acclaimed in his journal. This apart, each of Schubert's compositions was given rave review in his journal as it came out of the press. Schumann's enthusiasm and support, particularly for repeated performances of the 'Great', and its subsequent publication by *'Breitkopf & Harte*l' in 1849, naturally gave Schubert a stronghold on Leipzig, at that time the most active musical centre of Europe.

With the posthumous publication of Schubert's compositions, his music, particularly his songs, soon began to make waves outside his native Vienna. In Paris, they were introduced by the French opera singer and composer Adolphe Nourrit and became so popular that soon they became an integral part of the concerts of the *'Conservatoire de Paris'*[133]. In the autumn of 1833, the first French collection of Schubert's music containing six songs – *"Six melodies celebres paroles francaises par M. Belanger de F. Schubert"* ('Six melodies famous French words by Mr. Belanger F. Schubert') was published by Richault, with translation by Bélanger. A short time later, the same publisher issued *"Le roi des aulnes"* (*"Erlkönig"* by Goethe), also

---

[133] The *'Conservatoire de Paris'* ('Paris Conservatory) is a college of music and dance founded in 1795. The Conservatoire offers instruction in music and dance, drawing on the traditions of the "French School".

translated by Bélanger. In 1834 or 1835 Prilip published four new Schubert melodies translated by Sivol. About four years later, a larger collection of songs, with translation by Emil Deschamps, was published by Brandus.

Adolphe Nourrit

After 1840 Schubert's Lieder were published in large numbers, the principal translators being Emil Deschamps and Bélanger. Richault was among the most active publishers in the field, issuing no less than 367 melodies between the years 1840 and 1850, all translated by Belanger and some of them also appearing in Italian translation. This led the way to the *"Quarante mélodies de Schubert"* ('Forty Schubert Melodies') of Richault, Launer, etc, published by Brandus in 1849, to which the English music lovers are indebted for their first acquaintance with these treasures of life.

Some of Schubert's chamber music also became quite popular in Paris, through the playing of Tilmant, Urhan, and Alkan, and later of Alard and Franchomme.[134]

---

[134] Noske Frits, Bento Rita: *"French Song from Berlioz to Duparc: The Origin and Development of the Melodie"*, Translated by Rita Benton, Published by Dover Publications Inc., Mineola, New York, 1970, p. 26-27.

Like Schumann, Liszt was also beholden to Schubert's music. As a passionate admirer of Schubert, he sought to keep the flame alive by his transcriptions of the songs and waltzes. His transcriptions have contributed in a big way to introduce Schubert into many quarters where his compositions would otherwise have been a sealed book.

The list of Schubert's works, posthumously published, is long and one can, therefore, go on and on. It is now acknowledged that the treasure he left behind for the music lovers all over the world is huge -- so huge that no complete critical edition of Schubert's works exists on date; and one is not even sure if all his compositions have surfaced as yet.

So the saga of Franz Schubert is one of a miraculous comeback of a little known young composer in Vienna, the city of great maestros – one who was subject to gross neglect during his lifetime and died an untimely death, practically penniless --- one whose father and brother had to approach his friends, pupils and other members of the public for financial assistance to meet the cost of his medical attendance, and funeral expenses. It is a captivating tale of how simply on the strength of a dusky bundle of unpublished music papers -- valued at 8*s*. 6*d*. -- left behind at the time of his death, he came to be acknowledged later as one of the greatest composers of all time.

Schumann was right when he wrote, "[Schubert] *ought to have lived to see how celebrated he is today; it would have inspired him to his best.*"

Today, Schubert, the 'King of lied', shares the centre-stage of the world of music along with other great masters -- in a majestic style that only befits a king. Like the mythical phoenix, Schubert too seems to have been born again arising from his ashes to cast a magical charm through his spellbinding music, which the music world had failed to take note of in his earlier incarnation.

Chapter 21
"*Zentralfriedhof*" in Vienna: The final resting place of Franz Schubert

Before he died on 19 November 1828, Schubert's last wish was to be buried near Beethoven, whom he greatly revered.

Two days later, on 21 November, in deference to his last wish, Schubert was buried in the '*Währing* Cemetery' just three graves away from Beethoven. A monument with the bust of the composer was also erected over his grave in his honour.

But it did not remain as such for long. Interestingly, over the subsequent years, the sepulchre at Wahring where Schubert had originally been buried came to acquire a checkered trajectory.

In 1863, owing to dilapidation of the graves of both Beethoven and Schubert the "*Gesellschaft der Musikfreunde*" ('Society of Friends of Music in Vienna'') decided to repair the burial site at Währing. They exhumed the bodies of the two great composers and put these in a new and more robust zinc coffin before burying them again. The operation began on 12th October and was completed on the 13th. In course of the operation, a cast and a photograph of Schubert's skull and measurements of the principal bones of both the skeletons were taken. The lengths in Schubert's case were to those in Beethoven's as 27 to 29, which implies that Beethoven was 5 ft. 5 in. high, while Schubert was only 5 ft. and ½ an inch.

In 1873, the cemetery in Währing was declared closed. Later in 1925, it was converted into a park in 1925, called the "*Schubert Park*".

'*Währinger Schubertpark*' (Schubert Park, Währing)

Meanwhile, in 1870, the Viennese authorities had built the Vienna Central Cemetery -- "*Zentralfriedhof*" – a giant cemetery away from the city centre. The new cemetery, however, was not an immediate hit with the public, which is one reason the city authorities, in keeping with the classical music heritage of Vienna, decided to put in some "celebrity graves" to boost its attractiveness. This included establishing a little cluster of great composer graves for the likes Johann Strauss II, Brahms, Beethoven, and Schubert.

So in 1888, the graves of both Beethoven and Schubert were dug up again and their remains were transferred to Vienna Central Cemetery — the "*Zentralfriedhof*" -- where they remain buried next to Gluck, Johannes Brahms, Johann Strauss II, Hugo Wolf and other musical greats -- in what is called the "*Garden of Honor*".

Schubert's Grave at "Zentralfriedhof" (Vienna Central Cemetery)

Today, Schubert lies here, in the "Garden of Honour", at grave no. 28, while Beethoven is at grave no.29.

So at long last, the 'dying wish' of the young hapless Schubert was fulfilled --- as if by divine desire -- as the 'King of Lied' rests in peace by the side of the 'King of Harmony', Ludwig van Beethoven.

Chapter 22
The king is dead, long live the king!
Schubert immortalized after death

"Schubert Denkmal": At Stadtpark, Vienna

To pay homage to Schubert, in 1872, the *"Wiener Männergesang Verein"* ('Viennese Male Voice Choir') erected by subscription a *"Schubert Denkmal"* ('Schubert monument'), as a gift to the city, in Vienna's Stadtpark ('City Park'). Located right on the edge of the city centre, the park has a tranquil surrounding with ornamental trees, open meadows and even a river running through it.

To erect the statue, the choir raised the funds over a ten-year period, Most of the income came from fools' evenings and folk concerts. Other singing clubs also contributed to the financing. This led the great patron of the arts, Nikolaus Dumba, to note in his speech at the official unveiling on May 15th that:

> *"We built this statue stone by stone not from donations but through his songs."*

The painter, and a friend of Schubert, Moritz von Schwind, was responsible for the likeness of the portrayal. The design of the memorial was done by the famous Austrian sculptor Carl Kundmann best known for his works which adorn the area around the Ringstrasse, the beautiful boulevard that is home to many of Vienna's most famous sights and museums, as well as grand palaces and spacious parks.. The work was such a success that it earned Kundmann a professorship at the Academy of Fine Arts, Vienna where he taught until his retirement in 1909.

Schubert: At Vienna's Stadtpark

(The base & the reliefs were designed by Theophil Hansen, the sculpture and the design of the memorial by Carl Kundmann)

The statue of Schubert at Stadtpark is in Carrara marble[135] with the inscription *"Franz Schubert, seinem Andenken der Wiener Mannergesang Verein, 1872"* ('In the memory of Franz Schubert, Viennese Male Voice Choir', 1872) on it. It cost 42, 000 florins. The foundation stone was laid in 1868, in the presence of the Mayor of Vienna, Andreas Zelinka. and was unveiled on May 15, 1872.

The unveiling was attended by the Mayor of Vienna Cajetan von Felder, members of the Schubert family and associates. The speech was, as mentioned earlier, given by Nikolaus Dumba, a well-known

---

[135] 'Carrara marble' is a type of white or blue-grey marble popular for use in sculpture. It is quarried in the city of Carrara in the province of Massa and Carrara in the Lunigiana, the northernmost tip of modern-day Tuscany, Italy.

Carrara marble has been in use since the time of Ancient Rome. It was used for some of the most remarkable edifices of the world, such as, 'The Pantheon', 'Trajan's Column', 'Column of Marcus Aurelius', etc. It was also used in many sculptures of the Renaissance including Michelangelo's 'David' (1501–04), The "Pietà" (1498–1499), etc.

industrialist and patron of the arts. The statue shows Schubert sitting pensively, poised to put down notes on paper and just waiting for the right inspiration. The base of the statue has three reliefs designed by Theophil Hansen[136] dedicated to the themes -- musical imagination, instrumental music, and vocal music.[137][138]

Music, singing and imagination

Relief in front: 'The Fantasy'

---

[136] Theophil Hansen (13 July 1813 – 17 February 1891) was a Danish architect who later became an Austrian citizen. He became particularly well known for his buildings and structures in Athens and Vienna, and is considered an outstanding representative of Neoclassicism and Historicism.

[137] *"The Schubert Statue"*, Visiting Vienna. https://www.visitingvienna.com/sights/schubert-statue/

[138] *"Franz Schubert"* Kunst und Kultur in Wien. http://www.viennatouristguide.at/Ring/Denkmal_Bild/z_schubert.htm

Relief left: 'The instrumental music'   Relief right: 'The vocal music'

Chapter 23
Schubert's Footprints: Now Museums/Memorials in Vienna

While the likes of Beethoven and other celebrated Viennese masters were adopted sons of Vienna, Schubert was the city's true biological offspring. He was born there, died there, and – for most of his short life – lived and worked there. It is, therefore, no wonder that the Viennese gentry spared no pains to preserve his footprints throughout the city -- as museums and memorials -- to commemorate him and his musical genius. The list is long – so just a few of these are outlined below:

'Schubert Geburtshaus' ('Schubert's birthplace'), *Nussdorfer Strasse 54*

The house in the Alsergrund district, where Schubert was born on January 31, 1797 and spent the early part of his childhood, is still there – firmly inside the city limits now– and features the *'Schubert Geburtshaus'* museum ('Schubert's birthplace'), a 'must see' for all Schubert aficionados visiting the city of Vienna.

At the time Schubert was born, it was called "*Zum roten Krebsen*" (The Red Crab) and was situated in the Viennese suburb of *Himmelpfortgrund*. Here Schubert spent the first four and a half years of his childhood. The apartment of the large family consisted solely of one room and a "*Rauchkuchl*" (kitchen with open fire).

The entrance to the house takes the visitor into a beautiful gravel courtyard surrounded by wooden balconies, reminiscent of late 18th-century Vienna. The museum itself is up some stone stairs and gives a historical feeling with its bare wooden floors and low ceilings with whitewashed walls.

There is a tablet on the birthplace of Schubert, which was carried out by the *"Wiener Männergesang Verein"* ('Viennese Male Voice Choir'). The work was completed on October 7, 1858

The museum contains several portraits of Schubert to admire and a pair of his famous spectacles. There's another pair in the "Haus der Musik" ('House of Music') at *Seilerstätte* in Central Vienna.

'Schubert Geburtshaus': Schubert's birthplace in Vienna

Other highlights of the museum include:

(i) Music stations where one can sit and listen to some of his compositions;

(ii) (ii) Schubert's school reports from 1809 and 1812, as well as his exam results from 1814; 1st edition sheet music for his famous *'Erlkönig'* song, as well as originals and copies of various other compositions;

(iii) A piano owned by his brother Ignaz, the keys of which Schubert once induced to produce sounds that would later become his masterpieces;

Two of the rooms in the Schubert house are dedicated to the Austrian writer, poet, and painter Adalbert Stifter, the great contemporary of Franz Schubert.

***Lichtentaler Pfarrkirche (Marktgasse 40)* ['Schubert's Church']**

A short walk from *'Schubert Geburtshaus'* (Schubert's birthplace) would take a visitor to *"Lichtentaler Pfarrkirche"* ('The Lichtental Parish Church'), also known as *"Schubertkirche"* ('Schubert's church'). This is the parish church where Schubert was baptised.

'Schubertkirche' ('The Schubert church')

The foundation stone for *'Schubertkirche'* was laid by Emperor Charles VI in 1712. Since then, the church has survived an explosion at a nearby gunpowder facility, floods, the Napoleonic occupation of Vienna, and bombing raids during the Second World War.

Schubert's connection with this church began with his father, who married here in 1785 and ran the parish school. Schubert himself was born three streets away and was baptised in this church on 1 February 1797.

It was here Schubert received his first musical training, went on to sing in the choir, play the organ (which is on display), and compose several works for the church. In 1814, at age 17, he was commissioned to compose a *'missa solemnis'* (solemn mass) for the centenary of the church --- his first mass, namely, 'Mass No. 1 in F major' and conducted the first performance there on September 25, 1814. His later masses in 'G major, B-flat major, and C major were also composed for Lichtental Church, as well as other sacred music.

There is a plaque outside the Schubertkirche that commemorates Schubert's connection with this church.

Schubert Sterbewohnung ('Schubert's last residence'), *1040 Vienna, Kettenbrückengasse 6*

In late 1828, a sick Franz Schubert moved into his brother Ferdinand's apartment on the second floor of a brand new house on Kettenbrückengasse, now known as the *"Schubert Sterbewohnung"*.

'Schubert Sterbewohnung' - The house where Schubert died

Schubert died on November 19, 1828, in his brother Ferdinand's apartment. Like his birthplace, the *'Schubert Sterbewohnung' ('Schubert's last residence')* is also a small museum.

There is a tablet on the last residence of Schubert, which was put up by the *"Wiener Männergesang Verein"* ('Viennese Male Voice Choir'). The work was completed in November 1859.

Inside there are three rooms, with creaking wooden floors and whitewashed walls. Here he composed his last works, among them the song "The Shepherd on the Rock". There is something strangely absorbing about standing in the smallest room knowing that Schubert wrote his final letters and compositions here before he died.

The items on display in the museum include:

(i) A real lock of Schubert's hair;

(ii) a piano belonging to Ferdinand that Schubert also played during his stay in this apartment;

(iii) reproductions of original sheet music, including for *'Taubenpost'*, the

last song he wrote;

(iv) an original invite to the requiem mass;

(v) a copy of the letter Ferdinand wrote to his father quoting Schubert on

his deathbed, interpreting his exclamations as a wish to be buried next

to Beethoven – a wish that was duly granted;

(vi) a record of Schubert's estate, essentially just a few items of clothing

(and a mattress) that didn't even cover outstanding medical and funeral expenses.

A piano belonging to Ferdinand that Schubert also played

The museum is part of the second floor of the house and the other apartments are still occupied. So the museum entrance is like a "normal" house entrance. To enter, one has to ring the bell to open the door leading off the street. And then ring another bell to open the door inside the courtyard that leads up to the museum – where the composer spent the last days before he breathed his last. [139][140][141][142]

---

[139] Kreissle von Hellborn, Heinrich: *"The Life of Franz Schubert"*, Vol. 2, Edited and translated by Arthur D. Coleridge, Published by Cambridge University Press, Cambridge, UK, 2014, p. 141-151.

[140] Wikisource: *"A Dictionary of Music and Musicians"*, Vol. 3, en.wikisource.org, p. 364-368.

[141] Grove, Sir George: "Beethoven - Schubert – Mendelssohn", Published by Read Books, 15 March 2007.

[142] Youens, Susan: *"Schubert: Die Schöne Müllerin"*, Published by Cambridge University Press, 1992, p.2.

Chapter 24
Schubert - A century later

In 1897, Schubert's birth centenary was celebrated in style throughout the musical world marked by festivals and performances dedicated to his music. In Vienna, there were ten days of concerts, and the Emperor Franz Joseph gave a speech recognizing Schubert as one of Austria's favourite sons. Karlsruhe saw the first production of his opera *'Fierrabras'*

In 1928, a "Schubert Week" was observed in Europe and the United States to mark the centenary of the composer's death. Works by Schubert were performed in churches, in concert halls, and on radio stations.

A fictionalized account of Schubert's romantic life was portrayed in *'Das Dreimädlerlhaus'* ("The House of the Three Maidens"), a Viennese operetta with music by Franz Schubert. The story was adapted from the 1912 novel *"Schwammerl"* ('Mushroom') by the famous Austrian writer Rudolf Hans Bartsch. The original production opened on 15 January 1916, at the Raimundtheater in the Mariahilf district of Vienna and ran for over 650 performances in its original run in Austria and for hundreds more in Germany, followed by many successful revivals. It was later premiered in Paris on May 7, 1921 in a French adaptation by called *"Chanson d'amour"* ('Song of Love').

The operetta was a huge success in France, and soon an English language adaption opened on Broadway in Manhatan, New York as *'Blossom Time'*, with a new arrangement of Schubert's music by the Hungarian-born American composer Sigmund Romberg. This debuted at the Ambassador Theatre on September 29, 1921, where it ran for 592 performances; it was revived several times on Broadway over the next two decades.

In London, the operetta was called '*Lilac Time*', and it opened at the Lyric Theatre on the Shaftesbury Avenue in the City of Westminster on December 22, 1922 and ran for 626 performances.

Both the Broadway and West End versions toured extensively in subsequent decades and were frequently revived until the 1950s.

The operetta received productions in over 60 countries and was translated into numerous languages. By 1961, the piece was estimated to have played over 85,000 performances worldwide. It still receives occasional productions.

Even today, more than two hundred years after his demise, Schubert's chamber music continues to be popular. In a survey conducted by the ABC Classic FM radio station, operated by the Australian Broadcasting Corporation, in 2008, Schubert's chamber works dominated the field, with the '*Trout Quintet*' ranked first, the '*String Quintet in C major*' ranked second, and the '*Notturno in E-flat major*', Op. 148 (also called 'Adagio') for piano trio' ranked third. Furthermore, eight more of his chamber works were among the 100 top-ranked pieces

Schubert has also featured as a character in a number of films including "*Schubert's Dream of Spring*" (1931), "*Gently My Songs Entreat*" (1933), "*Serenade*" (1940), "*The Great Awakening*" (1941), "It's Only Love" (1947), "*Franz Schubert*" (1953), *Mit meinen heißen Tränen* (With my hot tears') (1986),. Schubert's music has also featured in numerous post-silent-era films, including Walt Disney's "*Fantasia*" (1940), which features "*Ave Maria*", D. 839.

In addition, Schubert's life was covered in the documentaries "*Franz Peter Schubert: The Greatest Love and the Greatest Sorrow*" by Christopher Nupen (1994), as well as in "*Schubert – The Wanderer*" by Andras Schiff and Mischa Scorer (1997), both produced for the BBC.

Schubert is also an important subject of scholarly pursuit in the academic world today, particularly in Europe. About two decades ago, the bicentenary celebrations of Franz Schubert's birth were held in Duisberg, Graz, Oxford, Paris and Vienna. The largest international gathering of Schubert scholars in recent times was held at Maynooth University, Ireland on 21–23 October 2011. The outcome of the scholarly discourse at these celebrations is a burgeoning literature in the field of Schubert studies. The wealth of research so published has greatly enhanced our understanding of Schubert's social circle as well as the contemporary historical and biographical issues, drawn attention to neglected repertoire and changed our perception of his compositional practice. More importantly, it has since begun to expand the academic focus beyond the domain of Schubert studies, quietly reorienting the erstwhile approaches and understanding of nineteenth-century music and culture.[143][144][145

----

[143] *"Franz Schubert: Biography, Music & Facts"*, Britannica.com

[144] *"Franz Schubert"*: Wikipedia

[145] Bodley, Lorraine Byme & Sobaskie, James William: "*Schubert Familiar and Unfamiliar: Continuing Conversations*", Nineteenth-Century Music Review, Cambridge University Press, Volume 13, Issue 1, June 2016, pp. 3-9.

Chapter 25
Epilogue

Today, as we think of Schubert's life and music, a feeling of tremendous loss and regret grips us. One wonders how much more the young master could have contributed to the world of music, if he had not died at an early age of 31. The great Romanian Pianist Radu Lupu, who shares the feeling, said:

> "[Schubert] *is the composer for whom I am really most sorry that he died so young. ... We'll never know in what direction he was going or would have gone.*"

There are, however, others who are of the opinion Schubert in his lifetime did produce enough masterpieces not to be limited to the image of an unfulfilled promise. In the opinion of Schumann, who is a strong proponent of this view, said: "*It is pointless to guess at what more [Schubert] might have achieved. He did enough; and let them be honoured who have striven and accomplished as he did*"

In a tribute to Schubert, the renowned Hungarian-born Austro-British classical pianist and conductor András Schiff said:

> "*Schubert lived a very short life, but it was a very concentrated life. In 31 years, he lived more than other people would live in 100 years, and it is needless to speculate what could he have written had he lived another 50 years. It's irrelevant, just like with Mozart; these are the two natural geniuses of music.*"

'The New York Times' has ranked Schubert as the fourth greatest composer of the world. Anthony Tommasini, the chief music critic of NY times, wrote of him:

Anthony Tommasini

"You have to love the guy, who died at 31, ill, impoverished and neglected except by a circle of friends who were in awe of his genius. For his hundreds of songs alone – including the haunting cycle Winterreise, which will never release its tenacious hold on singers and audiences – Schubert is central to our concert life... Schubert's first few symphonies may be works in progress. But the Unfinished and especially the Great C major Symphony are astonishing. The latter one paves the way for Bruckner and prefigures Mahler."

And so the legacy of Franz Schubert, the amazing composer, continues. Schubert tragically left this world leaving behind his prodigious output of spellbinding music -- without caring for prosperity, gain or, even the fate of his work. He was the tragedy prince of the world of music -- who died a sad and unhappy man -- without proper recognition of his sparkling genius. But yet his timeless music lives on --- everlasting and immortal -- for the generations to come.

References

1. Baltzell, Winton James: "*A Complete History of Music for Schools, Clubs, and Private Readings*", published by the Library of Alexandria, August 28, 2017.

2. Barnett, Laura, "*Arts Diary: Unfinished gets finished*". The Guardian, 11 July 2007.

3. "*Being There*". IMDb.

4. Bodley, Lorraine Byrne: "*Schubert's Goethe Settings*", published by Ashgate, 2003.

5. Bodley, Lorraine Byme & Sobaskie, James William: "*Schubert Familiar and Unfamiliar: Continuing Conversations*", Nineteenth-Century Music Review, Cambridge University Press, Volume 13, Issue 1, June 2016, pp. 3-9.

6. Bogousslavsky, Julien, Hennerici, M. G., Baezner, H., Bassetti, C. (Ed.): "*Neurological Disorders in Famous Artists*", Part 3, Karger, 2010, p. 76-77.

7. "*Boo Bop*". IMDb.

8. Clive, Peter: "*Schubert and His World: A Biographical Dictionary*", Clarendon Press, Oxford, 1997, p. 93.

9. Crowest, Frederick J (Ed.): "*Schubert*" in "*The Master Musicians*" series published by J. M. Dent & Co., 29 & 30, Bedford Street, W.C., 1905.

10. "*D-Verz.: 759, Titel: Sinfonie Nr.7* ". Neue Schubert-Ausgabe, Schubert-database.

11. DeVoto, Mark (2011). "*Background: Schubert's Great C Major: Biography of a Symphony*". Boydell and Brewer. pp. 1–12.

12. Duncan, Edmondstoune, *"Schubert"*. J. M. Dent & Co., 1905, p. 165.

13. Dvořák, Antonin: *"Franz Schubert"*, (in collaboration with Henry T. Finck), published in The Century Illustrated Monthly Magazine, New York, 1894

14. Ernst Hilmar: *"Franz Schubert""*. Rowohlt, Hamburg 1997, p. 97

15. Flower, Newman: *"Franz Schubert - The Man And His Circle"*, Tudor Publishing Co., New York, December, 1935.

16. *"Franz Schubert, Complete Symphonies, Robert Cummings"*. Bamberg Symphony, Jonathan Nott, Tudor 7141 Hybrid Multichannel SACD.

17. *"Franz Schubert"* Kunst und Kultur in Wien.

    http://www.viennatouristguide.at/Ring/Denkmal_Bild/z_schubert.htm

18. *"Franz Schubert: Biography, Music & Facts"*, Britannica.com

19. *"Franz Schubert: The Last Classical Composer and his Symphony No. 8 "Unfinished""*, The Classical Difference. https://www.classicaldifference.com/schubert/

20. Gibbs, Christopher H.: *"The Life of Schubert"*, Cambridge University Press, March 2015.

21. Greenberg, Robert: *"Music History Monday: Schubert's Death"*, Published in 'Medium Music' 19 November 2018.

22. Grove, Sir George: *"A Dictionary of Music and Musicians"*, Wiki source, p. 371.

    https://en.wikisource.org/wiki/Page:A_Dictionary_of_Music_and_Musicians_vol_3.djvu/371

23. Grove, George: *"Grove's Dictionary of Music and Musicians"*, Published by Franklin Classics Trade Press, 31 October, 2018.

24. Grove, George Sir: *"Beethoven – Schubert – Mendelssohn"*, Read Books, March 15, 2007.

25. Henahan Donal: *"Music View: The Dark Side of Schubert"*, published in 'The New York Times', August 27, 1989, The New York Times Archives.

26. Hetenyi, G.: *"The terminal illness of Franz Schubert and the treatment of syphilis in Vienna in the eighteen hundred and twenties"*.
https://www.utpjournals.press/doi/pdf/10.3138/cbmh.3.1.51

27. Ho, Desiree: *"Franz Schubert's Illness: The Melancholy of an Autumnal Sunset"*, Published in 'Interlude', 7 October 2011.

28. Horton, Julian (2015): *"Schubert"*, Routledge, p. 66.

29. Huizenga, Tom: *"Nikolaus Harnoncourt: Schubert's Religion"*, published in 'The NPR Music Newsletter', May 11, 2006.

30. Huscher, Philip: "*Program Notes: Schubert, Symphony No. 9*" Chicago Symphony Orchestra, 2012.

31. Johnson, Graham: *"Program notes to Schubert, Hagars Klage"*, Performed by Christine Brewer, soprano, Graham Johnson, piano. The Hyperion Schubert Edition, 31. London: Hyperion Records, CDJ33031, 1998.

32. Kasper, Peter Paul. *"Schubert und die Religion."* Singende Kirche 44, no. 3 (1997): 167–168.

33. Keller, James M.: *"Schubert: Symphony in C major, D.944, The Great"*, Program Notes, San Francisco Symphony, October 2017. https://shorturl.at/bIJOP

34. Kreissle von Hellborn, Heinrich: *"The Life of Franz Schubert, Vol. 1"*, Edited and Translated by Coleridge, Arthur Duke, Cambridge University Press, Cambridge, UK, 2014.

35. Kreissle von Hellborn, Heinrich: *"The Life of Franz Schubert"*, Vol. 2, Edited and translated by Arthur D. Coleridge, Published by Cambridge University Press, Cambridge, UK, 2014, p. 141-151.

36. *"Letter to Leopold Kupelwieser"*, March 31, 1824: Reprinted in "Music in the Romantic Era" by Alfred Einstein, W.W. Norton& Company, (1 April, 1947).

37. Lewis Jr., Joseph W.: *"Last and Near-Last Words of the Famous, Infamous and Those In-Between"*, published by Author House, 2016.

38. Maerk, George: *"Schubert"*, published by Viking Adult, 1 November 1991.

39. McCafferty, Megan: *"Charmed Thirds"*, Broadway Books, April 11, 2006.

40. Mirkin, Dr. Gabe: *"Franz Schubert, Syphilis and Mercury Poisoning"*.

41. https://shorturl.at/ajEK4

42. Moon, Jason Jye-Sung: *"A Guide to Franz Schubert's Religious Songs"*, Unpublished Dissertation submitted to the faculty of the Indiana University Jacobs School of Music in partial fulfillment of the requirements for the degree 'Doctor of Music' in Voice, December 2013, p.13.

43. *"Musical Terminology Glossary"* by Wikipedia.
https://www.translationdirectory.com/glossaries/glossary307.php

44. Newbould, Brian: *"Schubert and the Symphony: A New Perspective"*, Toccata Press, 1972

45. Newbould, Brian: *"Schubert Studies"*, Routledge. 16 June 2017.

46. Newbould, Brian: *"Schubert: The Music and the Man"*, University of California Press, Berkeley, Los Angeles, April 12, 1999.

47. Noske Frits, Bento Rita: *"French Song from Berlioz to Duparc: The Origin and Development of the Melodie"*, Translated by Rita Benton, Published by Dover Publications Inc., Mineola, New York, 1970, p. 26-27.

48. Oestreich, James R., "*Schubertizing the Movies*". The New York Times Company. 30 June 2002.

49. Pascall, Robert: *"Brahms & Schubert"*, The Musical Times, Vol. 124, No. 1683 (May, 1983), pp. 286-291.

50. *"Piano Sonata in G major, D 894 (Schubert)"*, Wikipedia.

51. Plantinga, Leon: *"Beethoven's Concertos: History, Style, Performance"*, New York: W.W. Norton, 1999.

52. Plutarch, '*The Life of Cimon*' [Plutarch: *"Six of Plutarch's Greek Lives: Cimon. Pericles, with the Funeral Oration of Pericles"*, Sagwan Press, 23 August 2015.

53. Richter, Goetz. "*Composers are under no threat from AI, if Huawei's finished Schubert symphony is a guide*". The Conversation.

54. Rolland, Romain: *"Beethoven"*, Published by Forgotten Books, 27 September 2018.

55. Sams, Eric: *"Schubert's Illness Re-Examined"*, The Musical Times, Vol. 121, No. 1643, January 1980.

56. Schoental, R.: *"The death of Schubert"*, Journal of the Royal Society of Medicine, Vol. 83, December, 1990, p.813.

57. Schumann, Robert von: *"Gesammelte Schriften Uber Musik Und Musiker"*, ('Collected Writings on Music and Musicians'), vol. ii, Georg Wigand's Verlag. ('George Wigand Publishing House'), 1854, p. 240.

58. Schuster, M. Lincoln: *"The World's Great Letters"*, Simon & Schuster Inc. New York City, New York, 1940, p. 266-267.

59. Schwarm, Betsy: *"Erlkönig, Song by Schubert"*, Encyclopedia Britannica.

60. Service, Tom: *"Symphony guide: Schubert's Ninth ('the Great')"*, The Guardian, 17 Jun 2014.

61. Shirley, Hugo. "*Stephen Hough; Orchestra of the Age of Enlightenment / Vladimir Jurowski, Weber: Freischütz Overture; Schubert: Symphony No.8 (compl. Safronov); Brahms: Piano Concerto No. 1, Royal Festival Hall, 6 November 2007*". MusicalCriticism.com.

62. Solomon, M.: "*Franz Schubert and the peacocks of Benvenuto Cellini*", 19th Century Music 12, 1989, p. 193–206.

63. Steblin, Rita, "*Schubert's Pepi: His Love Affair with the Chambermaid Josepha Pöckelhofer and Her Surprising Fate*". The Musical Times, 2008, p. 47–69.

64. Steblin, Rita: "*Schubert's Problematic Relationship with Johann Mayrhofer: New Documentary Evidence*". Barbara Haggh (ed.): Essays on Music and Culture in Honor of Herbert Kellman. Paris-Tours: Minerve, p. 465–495.

65. Steblin, Rita: "*The Peacock's Tale: Schubert's Sexuality Reconsidered*", 19th Century Music, Berkeley, California: University of California Press, 1993, p. 5-33

66. Stevenson, Joseph. "*Symphony No. 10 in D major (sketch), D. 936a*". The AllMusic guide. Retrieved 7 September 2013.

67. Susan Youens: *"Schubert – The Beautiful Miller"*. Cambridge University Press, 1992, p. 22.

68. "*Symphony No. 9 in C Major*", Written by Betsy Schwarm, Encyclopedia Britannica.

69. The Century Illustrated Monthly Magazine, Vol. XLVIII, No. 3 (July 1894), pp. 341–46).

70. *"The Poems of Goethe"* (1853), translated by Edgar Alfred Bowring, p. 99.

71. "*The Schubert Statue*", Visiting Vienna. https://www.visitingvienna.com/sights/schubert-statue/

72. Till Gerrit Waidelich: *"Unknown Schubert documents from Breslau"*. In: Schubert: Perspectives, 8, 2008, Stuttgart 2009, pp. 17–48,

73. Tomes, Susan: *"Out of Silence: A Pianist's Yearbook"*, The Boydell Press, Woodbridge, 2010, p. 147.

74. Wikipedia: *"The beautiful Miller"*

75. Wikisource: *"A Dictionary of Music and Musicians"*, Vol. 3, en.wikisource.org, p. 364-368.

76. Winter, Robert S.: *"Whose Schubert?"* 19th-Century Music, Vol. 17 No. 1, Summer, 1993; Published by University of California Press, p. 94-101.

77. Youens, Susan: *"Schubert: Die Schöne Müllerin"*, Published by Cambridge University Press, 1992, p.2.

78. Ziese, Elly: *"Schubert's death and burial in the oldest depiction"*, published by Gotland Vlg., Großdeuben, circa 1933.

………